Amesbury:
history and description of a south Wiltshire town

by

John Chandler
and
Peter Goodhugh

Amesbury: The Amesbury Society

1979

Published by The Amesbury Society,
34 Countess Road, Amesbury, Salisbury, Wiltshire

First published 1979
© John Howard Chandler and Peter Stephen Goodhugh, 1979

All rights reserved. No part of this publication may be reproduced, stored in a retrieval system, or transmitted, in any form or by any means, electronic, mechanical, photocopying, recording or otherwise, without the prior permission of the authors.

The maps in this publication are based upon the Ordnance Survey maps with the permission of the Controller of Her Majesty's Stationery Office.
Crown copyright reserved.

The endpaper photographs are reproduced by permission of Her Majesty's Stationery Office.
© Crown copyright 1979

The text of this book is set in 10pt Theme medium with headlines in 11pt Theme bold
by *Styleset Limited*, 23a New Street, Salisbury, Wiltshire

Printed by Press 70 Ltd., Volpoint House, Milford Industrial Estate, Salisbury, Wiltshire

Bound by Alamein Industries, Enham Alamein, Andover, Hampshire

I.S.B.N. 0 950 6643 0 8

This book is dedicated to the memory of

WILLIAM KEMM
JOB EDWARDS
LEONARD BUCKLAND

Historians of an earlier Amesbury

CONTENTS

FOREWORD

PART ONE. AMESBURY: A HISTORY *by John Chandler*

CHAPTER ONE: EARLY AMESBURY (to 979)   1
Introduction; The First Inhabitants; Vespasian's Camp; Saxon Amesbury before the Abbey

CHAPTER TWO: THE FIRST ABBEY (979–1177)   7
The Foundation of the Abbey; Domesday Amesbury; The End of the First Abbey

CHAPTER THREE: MEDIEVAL AMESBURY   12
The Priory; Pilgrims and Legends; The Medieval Town; The Dissolution

CHAPTER FOUR: LANDLORD, TENANT, AND LAND   22
The Squire; The Tenants; Agriculture

CHAPTER FIVE: THE TRADING TOWN (1539–1914)   30
The Clay Pipe Industry; Turnpikes and Stagecoaches; Shopkeepers and Tradesmen

CHAPTER SIX: SOCIAL CHANGE (1539–1914)   35
Poverty; Fires; Religion; Education; Into the Twentieth Century

PART TWO. AMESBURY: A TWENTIETH CENTURY SURVEY
by Peter Goodhugh

CHAPTER SEVEN: INTRODUCTION   43

CHAPTER EIGHT: THE APPROACHES TO THE VILLAGE   49
South (South Mill Hill, The Workhouse, South Mill, Amesbury Electric Light Company, Salisbury Road, Earls Court Road and Parsonage Lane); North (Countess Road); East (The Railway, Holders Road, Kitchener Road, The Drove and Coldharbour, The London Road); West (Stonehenge Road)

CHAPTER NINE: AMESBURY CHURCH   74
Introduction; The Exterior (The South Transept, The South Aisle, The Nave, The North Transept, The Chancel); The Interior (The South Transept, The South Aisle, The Nave, The North Transept, The Chancel, The Tower, The Saxon Cross, Bosses and Corbels); Conclusion

CHAPTER TEN: THE CENTRAL AREA   88
Recreation; Church Street; Manorial Life; High Street; The Centre; Smithfield Street; Flower Lane; Salisbury Street

NOTES AND SOURCES   127

BIBLIOGRAPHY   129

INDEX   132

FOREWORD

This book has grown out of a suggestion made some two years ago that, as one of the many ways in which Amesbury might celebrate its abbey's millennium, a souvenir history should be produced. The result is perhaps on a more ambitious scale then was originally intended, and the attentive reader may sometimes perceive the haste in which it has been written. Nevertheless we hope that it will prove of interest to both residents and visitors, whose appetites for Amesbury's past will have been whetted by the extensive programme of celebrations in the town during 1979.

As suggested by its title, this book falls into two distinct sections, a history and a description. The first six chapters, which form a short history of Amesbury before living memory, are the work of John Chandler. Peter Goodhugh has written a description of the town with illustrations from his collection of early photographs and postcards. This arrangement has led to some duplication and doubtless many omissions, but was nevertheless felt to be more useful to sightseer and student than a more integrated approach. Each author has benefited from the criticisms of the other, but each remains solely responsible for his own section. The maps have been drawn by Barry Keel, and Jim Hopkinson has helped with the reproduction of the photographs.

This project would not have been made possible without the help and kindness of many individuals and organisations. A principal regret is that some of those who gave initial inspiration were unable to see the finished work. Our first acknowledgement must be to the many present and former residents of Amesbury who provided detailed background information and the invaluable photographs. In particular: Olive Lady Antrobus, Sir Philip Antrobus Bt., The Antrobus Trustees, Betty Blake, Don Blakely, the late Ivor Buckland, Gerald Burden, Sam Dimer, Freda Dudek, Marjorie Dunford, Harold Eyres, Ralph Eyres, Olive Holmes, Phylis Hunt, Roselle Jones, Leslie Keel, Doris Lawrence, Jesse Lawrence, Olive Lawrence, Margaret Pethybridge, Frank Piesing, May Revett, Edmund Sandell, Kathleen Sims, Edward Snook, Alfred Southey, Alice Todd, Austin Underwood, Florence Williams, and the firms of Amesbury Motor Cycles and T. L. Fuller & Sons.

In addition, it is our pleasant duty to acknowledge the following debts of gratitude: to the unfailingly courteous staff of the Wiltshire Record Office and Salisbury Diocesan Record Office; to the late (and sadly missed) Richard Sandell, honorary librarian of the Wiltshire Archaeological and Natural History Society; to Peter Saunders and his staff at the Salisbury and South Wiltshire Museum; to members of the staff of Wiltshire Library and Museum Service, especially Edward Boyle, Jane Butterworth, Michael Corfield and Rosemary Green; to the librarians of the Universities of Bristol and Southampton; to the librarian of Dr. Williams' Library for allowing access to the Evans manuscript; to Country Life magazine; to the Keeper of Public Records; to A. & A.E.E. Boscombe Down; to Desmond Bonney of the Royal Commission on Historical Monuments (England), Salisbury; to Robert Gates of Press 70; to the Amesbury Parish Council for its generous help towards the cost of publication; to Peter Ball, John Buffrey, Roy Canham, Marjorie Dunford and Peter Nicholson, who have read and commented upon parts of the work in typescript; to Ann and Christine, our long-suffering wives.

J.H.C.
P.S.G.
Feast of Saint Melor May 1979

AMESBURY: A HISTORY

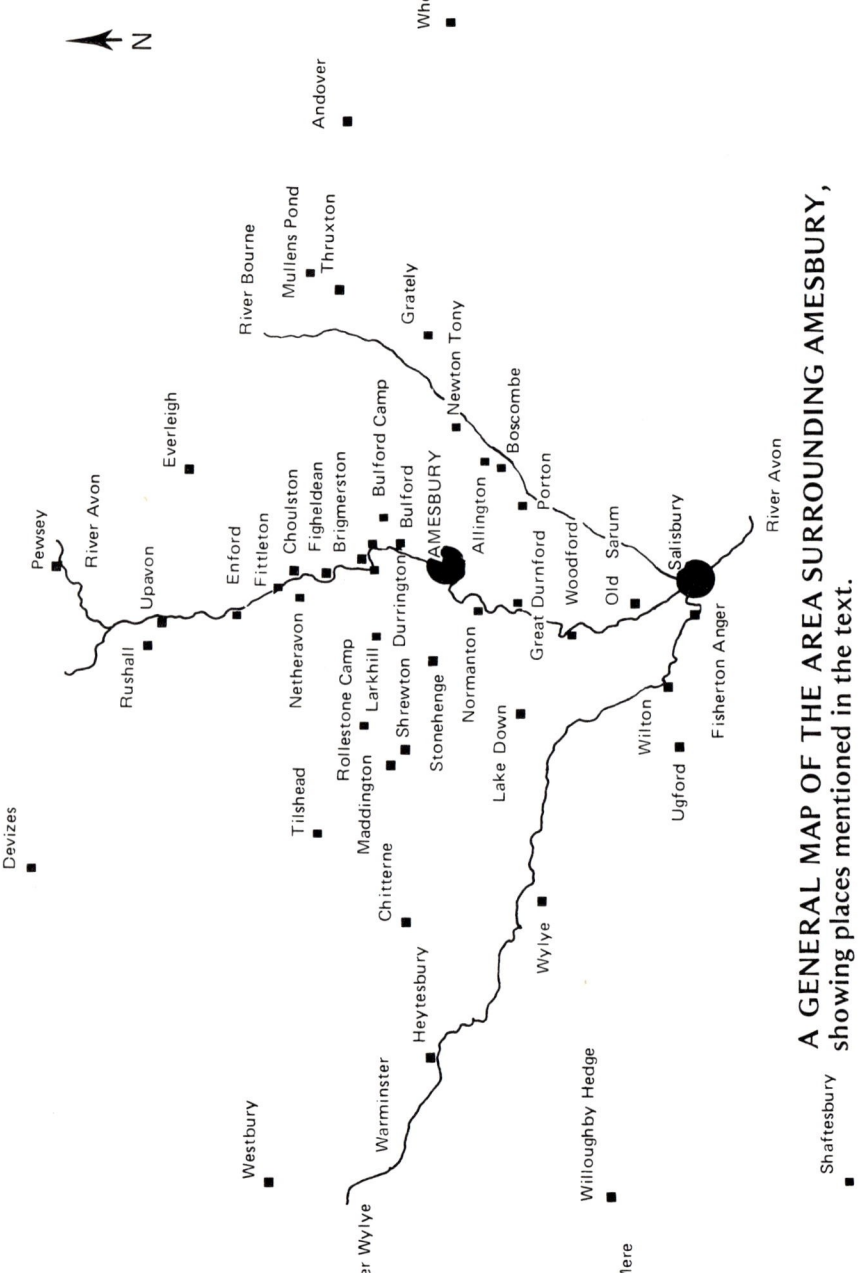

A GENERAL MAP OF THE AREA SURROUNDING AMESBURY, showing places mentioned in the text.

CHAPTER ONE: EARLY AMESBURY (to 979)

Introduction

The subject of this affectionate biography is a small Wiltshire town. Amesbury lies on a meander of the River Avon, eight miles north of Salisbury, at a point where the main road from London to Exeter bridges the river. The chalk downlands of Salisbury Plain surround the town, pocked with remains of earlier civilisations. Until the present century Amesbury depended on agriculture, but now its five thousand inhabitants look mostly to the neighbouring service establishments or to Salisbury for their employment. The nucleus of the town and its medieval abbey church remain, although the 'great thoroughfare' which once formed the High Street has been channelled into a modern by-pass. The abbey mansion has been divided into flats, the eighteenth century houses of the town centre are interspersed with petrol stations, and modern housing estates have encroached onto the common fields. Amesbury may not impress the casual visitor, or even the resident, with a sense of history in the way that Salisbury (an altogether younger place) does, but there is plenty in Amesbury's past that deserves to be remembered.

In fact it would be impossible in a few pages to do justice to the thousand years of history which separate the abbey foundation from today, and which Amesbury, in 1979, is celebrating. Instead this essay examines some of the subjects which seemed to the writer to be the most important in the town's past or the most interesting for the town's present. A great deal remains to be discovered about Amesbury; it is to be hoped that others will be inspired by the shortcomings of this essay to embark on studies of their own.

The First Inhabitants

The foundation of the first abbey in 979 was a landmark in the history of Amesbury, but it does not mark the beginning of the town. The first and most basic of questions, "How old is Amesbury?" cannot be answered by a simple date, and it is by no means easy to know where to begin this history.

And yet we must answer the question and begin at the beginning. Before the beginning, in fact, the River Avon meandered through the wooded valley beneath the chalk downs. To the first nomadic inhabitants of Wessex a river meant water for sustenance but an obstacle to be forded. Casual finds suggest occupation in mesolithic and neolithic times to the north of Amesbury, in the vicinity of Totterdown and Woodhenge, which may reflect an early fording-place, and the

Harrow Way, a trackway of venerable antiquity, forded the river at Ratfyn, also north of Amesbury. To the neolithic settlers of about 3400—2000 before Christ we owe the long barrows and the cursus, a linear earthwork more than two kilometres long to the north of Stonehenge. This, and the bank and ditch henge monuments which were constructed towards the end of the neolithic period, must have required a huge workforce and suggest a fairly large population of semi-nomadic farmers in the area.

A new element in the economy of Salisbury Plain came with the arrival of immigrants from the Rhineland (beaker culture) who brought with them knowledge of bronze-working and established a trade route from Ireland to the Continent, through Wales and southern England. Taking over the henge monuments from their predecessors they embellished Stonehenge with a double bluestone circle from the Prescelly Mountains of south Wales and erected timber structures in Durrington Walls. Many of the round barrows in the vicinity of Stonehenge were built to contain the remains of members of this culture.

The height of prosperity was reached perhaps between 1600 and 1400 B.C. during the period of the so-called 'Wessex culture' (which combined elements of the beaker culture newcomers and their neolithic predecessors). Now the sarsen trilithons were dragged from the Marlborough Downs and the richest of the barrow burials took place, many in Amesbury parish within sight of Stonehenge, which the wealth of their occupants had helped to create. The few square miles of downland which now overlook Amesbury must have enjoyed fame and national importance at this period such as the town of Amesbury has never achieved. And yet these wealthy traders and farmers, populous though the area was, appear not to have formed permanent settlements but retained their semi-nomadic or transhumant way of life, congregating at the landmarks they had created only for the purposes of religion and business.

Several centuries were to pass, and with them the glories of the Stonehenge builders, before bronze age society became more settled, with emphasis being placed for the first time on land divisions and territorial boundaries. Nearly thirty field systems, of various sizes, have been identified on either side of the River Avon between Upavon and Woodford, and although most cannot be dated as early as the late bronze age, the important 600 hectare site on the downs above Figheldean, Brigmerston and Milston has yielded late bronze age material, and it is to be supposed that many other field systems, whether still existing or now obliterated by later cultivation, were in use at this time. Pastoral enclosures have been discovered, but, like the field systems, they tended to exist on the downs overlooking the river valley rather than in the valley itself, which was probably dense forest in most places. As yet, apart from a few bronze age barrows in the vicinity of Vespasian's Camp, there is little to suggest that the site of present-day Amesbury was occupied to any extent, either in the centuries of the construction of Stonehenge, or during the remainder of the bronze age. Thus, to return to the original question, we may reply that, although the Amesbury area was comparatively densely populated in neolithic and bronze age times, and was indeed for a while the centre of the prehistoric world, Amesbury itself, as a community, had not yet begun.

Vespasian's Camp

If we are looking for the first Amesbury we must turn our attention to Vespasian's Camp. Vespasian's Camp is a large (about sixteen hectares) iron age hillfort lying immediately opposite modern Amesbury on the west bank of the river. In plan it forms an elongated triangle pointing north, with an extension to the south to meet the meandering river. To the naturally steep west and north-east sides of the spur was added a single bank and ditch, and at the northern tip, where the trackway known as the Harrow Way passed close by, an entrance was made. A second entrance may have existed in the south-east corner, where the modern Stonehenge Road enters the site. Its title is a product of eighteenth century antiquarianism and a complete misnomer—Vespasian would have been a most unwelcome visitor to this camp! No archaeological excavation of the hillfort has ever taken place, so its period of occupation and the nature of its economy remain unknown; (recent sectioning of the defences during road-widening, however, suggested that the fortifications fell into two phases). Certain observations may be made based on analogy with excavated sites, its size and its position.

Most hillforts were probably constructed within a few centuries of 500 B.C.; at first a single bank and ditch were built to fortify a natural stonghold, and later second and third banks were added to some of the more important sites. No rigid division may be drawn between the pastoral settlers of the late bronze age and the hillfort builders, although it is clear that a change in the social structure was taking place. There was now a need for defence from attackers, and—more important—there was now once again a sufficiently strong tribal authority to organise the enormous corporate labour involved. The hillfort dwellers continued to farm the land of their ancestors, and extensive remains of their agriculture, in the form of field boundaries, ditches and enclosures, are visible from air photographs of Earls Farm Down and elsewhere. During the more perilous periods of the iron age these farmers probably made their homes within the ramparts of Vespasian's Camp, in streets of circular wooden huts; in less troubled times, however, they may have lived in homesteads near their fields (a settlement site is known to have existed on South Mill Hill), and used the hillfort only as a temporary refuge.

By analogy with hillforts which have been thoroughly excavated, it has been calculated that a fort of the size of Vespasian's Camp could have enclosed a population approaching one thousand. A considerable tract of cultivated land would have been necessary to support so populous a village, and this raises the interesting, if speculative, question of the hillfort's territory and its relationship with neighbouring communities. The absence of hillforts on the plain to the north-west of Vespasian's Camp is notable, and this downland was probably used to graze the shorthorn cattle and small iron age sheep which manured the arable. Ogbury Camp, an enormous hillfort-type enclosure near Great Durnford, was probably a cattlefold and, because of its proximity to Amesbury, may have been used by the inhabitants of Vespasian's Camp. Next to the south lies Old Sarum, a very important settlement, and it may be that, by the time of the Roman invasion, this fort had eclipsed Vespasian's Camp (many hillforts had been abandoned by this time) and controlled all the Avon Valley from Bulford to Fisherton Anger.

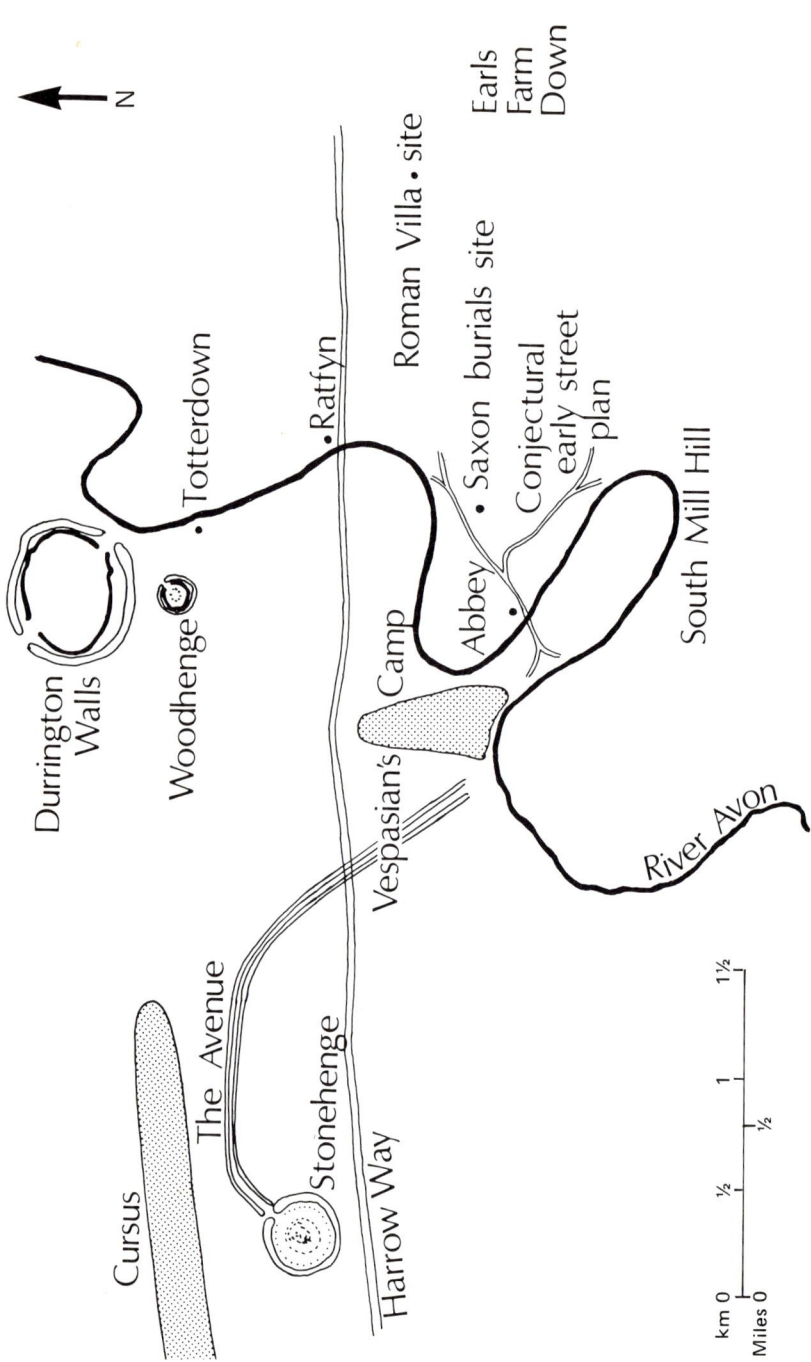

PRINCIPAL ARCHAEOLOGICAL SITES NEAR AMESBURY

In 43 A.D. four Roman legions invaded Britain and one, under the future emperor Vespasian, was employed in knocking out native strongholds in Wessex and the south-west peninsula. There is no evidence that Vespasian's Camp was one of the twenty hillforts which his biographer claims him as conqueror, but it has been suggested that one line of penetration may have been up the Avon valley and along the Vale of Pewsey towards the Bristol region. Evidence for this is provided by stray finds of Roman weaponry at Wilsford and Bulford, but there is no indication whether the occupants of Vespasian's Camp (if indeed it was still occupied) resisted the Roman advance or surrendered without a struggle.

Meanwhile, and throughout the Roman period, we must imagine that the fields of Amesbury continued to be cultivated, as the native iron age farmers came under the influence of Rome. There is ample evidence of activity in the Amesbury area during the Roman period, and villa settlements have been discovered on Earl's Farm Down and near Durrington Walls. Under Roman rule the dangers which had prompted the fortification of Vespasian's Camp had largely disappeared, and the site was probably abandoned until such time as it might be needed again.

Saxon Amesbury Before the Abbey

Settlement in the Amesbury area probably continued after the collapse of Roman rule and into the confused anarchy of the fifth century. Life in the villa on Earl's Farm Down was perhaps still possible, and the inhabitants of the valley may have continued to rely on the villa-owner for their livelihood. But as the systems of trade and currency collapsed and law and order disappeared the community was forced to depend entirely on itself; the survivors probably returned to Vespasian's Camp, the refuge of their ancestors, to farm the surrounding land by day and shelter in the safety of the ramparts at night. In this manner life may have continued at Amesbury until the mid-sixth century, but then a crucial change occurred.

In 552, according to the Anglo-Saxon Chronicle, Saxon invaders penetrated the coastal area of the Solent and defeated the indigenous population at Old Sarum. Their victory left them free to colonise the river valleys which converge on Salisbury, and it is likely that the first Saxon settlement at Amesbury took place about this time. Evidence of occupation during the following two centuries is meagre and is based on archaeological finds and place-name considerations.

The earliest forms of the name Amesbury—'Ambresbyrig' and 'Amberesburg' —although themselves dating from the eleventh century, hint that the name may be of sixth or seventh century origin. The second element clearly refers to the 'burh' or 'stronghold' of Vespasian's Camp, an indication that it was still strategically important. The first element is probably the personal name of the owner, 'Ambri' or 'Ambre', although another suggestion has been made that it refers to a detachment of the troops of Ambrosius Aurelianus, the semi-legendary British hero, which may have been garrisoned in the hillfort.

The most important archaeological evidence of this, the pagan Saxon period, is unfortunately not substantiated. In about 1835, during the demolition of a house at the bottom of London Road, Amesbury, several Saxon burials with seaxes (knives or daggers) are reported to have been uncovered. Other interments of the period, intrusive burials in bronze age barrows, have also been discovered from time to time, in particular a barrow on Boscombe Down West excavated in 1930. A further indication of pagan Saxon occupation may be provided by the place-name Haradon Hill, which is taken to derive from 'hearg', a heathen temple. If this is correct, the name would have been coined at the end of the pagan Saxon period, perhaps about 700 A.D., when the survival of a heathen temple was exceptional.

Thus by the eighth century there is evidence of settlement on both banks of the Avon at Amesbury, and therefore of a river-crossing between them. In the next two centuries, up to the foundation of the first abbey, the community grew in importance and became a royal manor, one of seven later known to have existed in Wiltshire. Archaeological excavation of derelict sites in the centre of Amesbury might provide invaluable information about this period of the town's expansion, but in its absence there is only conjecture.

There can be little doubt that by the time of the first abbey's foundation, about 979, Amesbury was of sufficient importance to have taken on the characteristics of a Saxon town. A street pattern would have begun to develop, with roads leading from the river-crossing to neighbouring settlements on either bank upstream and downstream. The first street plan may have evolved in the form of a 'T', Salisbury Street forming the upright stroke and Church Street and High Street the cross-pieces. Each road perhaps forked into two lanes at the edge of the settlement. It is a sign of greater confidence in the political stability of Wessex that the focus of settlement crossed the river from the fortified 'Ambresburh' to the more spacious, but vulnerable, left bank.

Royal ownership of Amesbury, which can be traced back to about 800, marked Amesbury out as a potential urban centre amid the welter of village settlements dotted along both banks of the river valleys. Their status afforded the inhabitants of Amesbury privilege and obligations, including a commitment to provide overnight hospitality for the king and his court when called upon to do so, as on the two occasions when the Witan, or assembly, met in the town. But more important for the prosperity of the town was the presence of the king's reeve. To him the surrounding villages brought their taxes in the form of produce, and at his hands they received justice. Thus Amesbury was to begin its career as an administrative and judicial centre, an importance which was later reflected in the hundred which it came to control and which bore its name.

Such is the picture of Amesbury before the abbey. Earlier historians have sometimes drawn on the legends of Melor, Ambrosius and Guinevere to embellish their accounts of this period. These legends, so far as they concerned Amesbury, originated towards the end of the medieval period, however, and it is best that we discuss them in that context.

CHAPTER TWO: THE FIRST ABBEY (979–1177)

The Foundation of the Abbey

The monastic ideal was not new in the tenth century. Religious communities had existed on the Continent since the later Roman empire and were established in Britain by Augustine and his seventh century successors. By the end of the ninth century, however, British monasticism was moribund, and the leaders of the tenth century monastic revival, Aethelstan, Edgar and archbishop Dunstan, adopted completely new sites for many of their foundations. Edgar, whose peaceful reign lasted from 959–975, was a fervent champion of the new monasticism and his views were shared by his second wife, Aelfthryth (Elfrida), who survived him. Edgar's death in 975, before either of his surviving sons had reached manhood, brought about a crisis. The succession passed to Edward, Edgar's son by his first wife, but his sovereignty was contested by supporters of Aethelred, Edgar's son by Aelfthryth. Edward's unpopular reign was turbulent but brief; in 978 he was murdered at Corfe Castle whilst visiting his stepmother, Aelfthryth, and the crown passed to her son, Aethelred, then a boy of about thirteen. Aelfthryth herself can hardly be held responsible for a murder in such embarrassing circumstances; for, whilst she doubtless preferred Edward dead, his blood spilled in her castle gave Aethelred's reign the most inauspicious of beginnings.

The foundation of nunneries at Wherwell near Andover and at Amesbury took place shortly after the assassination, probably therefore in 979. The traditional reason for the foundation, Aelfthryth's penance for the murder of her stepson, can be no more than partly true, especially if as seems likely she was not herself guilty of the treachery. In so far as an act of contrition was necessary, on a political level, in order that the new regime might appear penitent for the heinous crime of its supporters, the tradition is doubtless correct. Edward had not been popular, and did not come to be venerated for a generation, but for the manner of his death his successor required the nation's forgiveness. There was, however, a second reason for the foundations. When Edward acceded to the throne in 975 he made it very plain that his father's policy of encouraging monasteries was at an end. During his short reign some communities may have been dispersed and others lost possessions; monasteries may even have been destroyed. The deliberate foundation of two monastic houses at the beginning of Aethelred's reign may be seen as a reaction to Edward's policy, a bold assertion by a new regime that it heralded the return of the stability and pro-monastic spirit of Edgar's government.

It is tempting to see the choice of Amesbury as a monastic foundation as in some way connected with the cult of St Melor, to whom, from a very early date, the church has been dedicated. The legend of Melor, which embodies several semi-historical Breton figures, tells of a young prince who was mutilated and later murdered by a wicked uncle to prevent his succession to the throne.

When miracles began to occur about his body and severed head his relics were venerated and he took his place in the canon of saints. (Later developments of the legend are discussed below in chapter three.) The relics of Melor probably came to Britain in the first half of the tenth century when many Breton saints were dispersed before invading hordes and their relics found their way to Wessex, whose king, Aethelstan, had close links with Brittany. On the strength of this and the close correspondence between the careers of Melor and Edward it has sometimes been suggested that a cult of Melor existed at Amesbury before 979 and that it was because of its existence that Aelfthryth chose Amesbury as the site of her new abbey.

Such an explanation raises more problems than it solves. Why, for instance, should the relics of Melor have been at Amesbury in the first place? And in any case such an explanation is not necessary to an understanding of why Amesbury was chosen as the site of a new abbey. Amesbury, as we have seen, was a thriving community at an important fording-point, in the heartland of old Wessex, which was already noted for famous nunneries (such as Shaftesbury, Wilton, Romsey and Winchester). It was also a royal estate (and had been since at least the time of Alfred) and so land was readily available to endow the new monastery. But apart from the general suitability of Amesbury without Melor, there is a very grave objection to the Melor theory. At the time of the foundation of Amesbury abbey Edward had not been venerated; indeed if the foundation preceded the translation of Edward's body to Shaftesbury in 980 the miracles which eventually led to his being styled St Edward the Martyr had probably not even begun. Even if they had, it was certainly not in Aelfthryth's interest to draw attention to the similarity between Edward and Melor, since she would thereby have glorified her hated stepson and cast herself in the role of Melor's wicked uncle. If, on the other hand, it was Melor who later came to be associated, in the eleventh century, with the recently venerated Edward, the otherwise inexplicable connection between Melor and Amesbury is easily explained, and the whole sequence is plausible. Thus it would appear that the relics of Melor came to Amesbury after the foundation rather than preceding it.

Domesday Amesbury

There is at present no evidence of the site of the original abbey buildings. A so-called 'Saxon' column, discovered about 1900 embedded in the eastern end of the nave north wall of the parish church, is now thought to be no earlier than the twelfth century, and not, therefore, a part of Aelfthryth's foundation. Indeed, the original buildings were probably constructed of wood, as at Wilton. However, the reworking of several Norman features in the present church, including the 'Saxon' column, is a clear indication that a building existed on this site before the dissolution of the first abbey in 1177. It is therefore probable that the original abbey complex was on or near the site of the present church.

The presence of a royally-endowed monastery at Amesbury should have provided a stimulus to the town's development. The arrival of Melor's relics should also have ensured the abbey's success. But, although the abbey was doubtless an asset, Amesbury's growth seems to been checked during the eleventh century. The abbey's income remained small, so that it ranked as one of the poorest nunneries in the country. The abbess never attracted any new endowments, nor did she acquire land (and with it influence) in Amesbury itself. Furthermore, Amesbury found that the ancient status which it had enjoyed, by virtue of being a royal village, had largely disappeared once the formerly peripatetic court had become more centralised. It had never in fact been of value to the crown as a revenue-earning estate; and its sole use, as a source of provisions, was now superseded. Many similar royal estates, by the time of the conquest, had been granted burghal status, which conferred on them the right to mint coins, build fortifications and perform a number of trading functions. But not so Amesbury, which thereby stood to suffer from the prosperity of neighbouring burhs, such as Tilshead and Bedwyn, royal manors which had formerly been of no greater importance than Amesbury.

At the time of the Norman conquest, therefore, Amesbury was something between a village and a town, owned by the king although dominated by a monastery, head of a hundred although not a burh. Some idea of life in Amesbury soon after the conquest may be gained from the Domesday Survey, compiled for William I in 1086. The principal entry for Amesbury begins as follows:

The king holds Amblesberie. King Edward held it. It never paid geld, nor was it assessed in hides. There is land for forty ploughs. In demesne are sixteen ploughs and fifty-five serfs and two coliberts. There are eighty-five villeins and fifty-six bordars having twenty-three ploughs. There are eight mills paying £4 10s and seventy acres of meadow. The pasture is four leagues long and three leagues broad. The woodland is six leagues long and four leagues broad.

Quite apart from its strange terminology Domesday has many pitfalls. As a royal manor Amesbury's possessions were scattered, and it is not certain that the totals given refer exclusively to the community in Amesbury itself. It has been noted also that some figures are approximate, and that even so the units of measurement are flexible. Nonetheless, Domesday is invaluable as a source of information about population and economic activity and as a means of comparison.

The different classes of society are shown clearly by the extract quoted above. Land held directly by the crown (in demesne) was farmed by slaves (serfs) and half-free men (coliberts) and this accounted for nearly half of Amesbury's arable land. The remainder was rented to villagers (villeins) and their social inferiors, cottagers (bordars). The figures for these two groups represent families, not individuals, and so each may represent three, four, or more inhabitants. Taking this into account, along with the few tenants of Amesbury lands not held by the crown, and the members of the monastic community, a figure of about seven hundred may very guardedly be suggested for the total population of Amesbury. On this basis Bedwyn would have been approximately the same size, Tilshead slightly smaller, and two nearby villages on the Avon—Durnford and Netheravon—rather less than half the size of Amesbury.

Land is divided in Domesday into four categories, arable (ploughland), meadow, pasture and woodland. By comparison with the other royal manors in Wiltshire Amesbury's quota of arable land was small whilst its woodlands were very large, a sign perhaps that forest clearance had taken place more slowly here than elsewhere. The number of mills, eight, may seem surprising, and it is rather higher than the average for Wiltshire, but no higher than the other royal manors. The river valleys of south Wiltshire, in fact, boast some of the highest concentrations of water-mills anywhere, and Amesbury's eight are not exceptional.

The typical Norman community, as depicted in Domesday, was largely self-supporting. Certain commodities, such as salt, had to be obtained from elsewhere, but by and large a village prospered according to the use it made of its land. Amesbury may have been able to earn some additional revenue from trade, since it was situated on a main road, was an administrative centre, and lay outside the gates of an abbey. The king's lands were not assessed for the tax known as geld, and so it is hard to see what effect the conquest had on the value of the manor; the single hide in Amesbury owned by Osmund, however, seems to have prospered, since in 1086 it is assessed at double its value in 1065.

The End of the First Abbey

The first abbey was a house of Benedictine nuns. Until the reforming orders of the twelfth century and later, which preferred new, isolated sites, most monasteries in England followed the Benedictine rule, and many were established in towns and cities, where they played no mean part in the life of their surroundings. Surprisingly little is known of the two hundred year history (979–1177) of the first abbey, so that any reconstruction must be based to some extent on conjecture.

Whether the original buildings were stonebuilt or wooden is unknown, but they are likely to have consisted of a small, possibly apsidal, church with a cloister surrounded by the conventual buildings. An infirmary perhaps also existed, separated from the other buildings. Assuming that the Norman work in the present church belonged to the church of the first abbey, it is clear that rebuilding took place at the end of, or after, the Norman period. This is seen in the nave, where the exterior north wall exhibits blocked Norman clerestory windows above the roof line of a former north aisle or cloister. There is no indication now, however, of either the length of the twelfth century nave or the size of the cloister.

From Domesday we learn that the abbess owned lands in several neighbouring villages, Bulford, Boscombe, Allington, Choulston, (near Figheldean) and Maddington, as well as a manor in Winterbourne Bassett (north Wiltshire) and lands in Berkshire. The latter may not have been a part of the original endowment but later additions, acquired on the dissolution of an early monastery at Kintbury. Compared with the two other Wiltshire Benedictine houses, Wilton and Malmesbury, Amesbury's income from its estates was small, about one fifth that of Wilton and one sixth that of Malmesbury. It seems also to have been vulnerable to encroachment from other landowners, since during the reign of Edward the Confessor two hides in Amesbury had been granted to the abbess of Wilton, and in 1086 the abbey had unjustly lost its holdings at Winterslow. The poverty of the house by comparison with its rivals, and the effect this had on limiting the town's development, should not however lead us to underestimate the importance of the abbey as a source of income and renown to the whole community. Nor should we imagine that the life of the nuns was anything but luxury compared with the squalor of the unfree townspeople outside their gates.

The first abbey ended as it had begun, in an act of political penance for a murder, in this case the murder of Thomas Becket. On the pretext of irregular living by the nuns, Henry II appropriated the abbey in 1177 so that he could endow a new foundation and thereby fulfil his vow at the shrine of Becket. The charge against the nuns was doubtless trumped up (the canons of Waltham Abbey, Essex, suffered in exactly the same way); it was never difficult to turn malicious gossip to good advantage. And yet it is certainly true that the Benedictine rule, as observed in the twelfth century, appeared to many to be too lax, and hence the movement in favour of new orders, such as that of the nuns of Font Evrault, to whom Amesbury Abbey now passed. In 1177 there were thirty nuns at Amesbury; all appear to have declined an invitation to join their more rigorous successors and were expelled. The abbess, Beatrice, was deposed and pensioned off.

CHAPTER THREE: MEDIEVAL AMESBURY

The Priory

The decision of the reigning monarch to suppress a mediocre house of nuns and replace it with a lavishly-endowed, splendid new priory of the fashionable Fontevraldine order marks Henry II as one of Amesbury's greatest benefactors. The year 1177, when the decision was taken, is therefore a crucial turning-point in the town's history. In May of that year the king in person saw the first community from the French mother house of Font Evrault installed at the abbey by the archbishop of Canterbury. Ten years later, after grants of land or churches in more than twenty parishes, and very extensive building operations to suit the nuns' spiritual and temporal needs, the new priory was complete, and the opening took place on 30th November 1186.

Amesbury was the fourth and last English house of the order of Font Evrault to be established. It was also the largest. The order differed from all other monastic orders (except Gilbertine) in admitting both male and female religious into one community, although the sexes were segregated by building separate conventual buildings, and the women, the prioress in particular, were always the more influential. Double houses, as these communities were called, sprang up in the twelfth century and met with mixed success; many, including Amesbury, eventually reverted to single houses.

For the time being Amesbury priory prospered. Various extensions and improvements to the fabric were made in the early thirteenth century. Royal patronage continued, and in 1285 two women of the royal family, Mary (Edward I's daughter) and Eleanor of Provence (his mother) entered the community; the king paid repeated visits to Amesbury. By 1317/8 the strength of the priory was 117 nuns and 20 male religious. Ten years later, at a service on Ascension Day, 1327, thirty-six nuns were consecrated, including the noble Isabel of Lancaster.

There were two flaws, however, in the structure of the priory. The first was a weakness in the Fontevraldine ideal of double houses, which led to tensions between the prioress and her subordinate prior. The second was the vulnerability of an alien priory when England was at war with the country of the mother house, in this case France. Amesbury owed allegiance to Font Evrault, and through Font Evrault to the pope himself. The priory therefore stood outside, in large measure, the control of the English secular and ecclesiastical administrations, and was open to reprisals from them in times of war. At Amesbury these manifested themselves in the form of disputes over the succession, the severing of some lines of communication with Font Evrauld, and attempts at confiscation.

Crisis point was reached in 1400. A dispute had arisen between the prioress, Sybil Montague (whose appointment and subsequent conduct seem to have been unsatisfactory). and the prior, Robert Dawbeney. After arbitration the matter was not finally resolved, and on 14th March 1400 a group of Dawbeney's supporters, encouraged by some brethren and nuns, imprisoned the prioress and held her hostage for several days inside the convent. Sybil was eventually restored to her position as prioress after a commission of enquiry, but the damage was irreparable. Font Evrauld took no part in the dispute, and it appears that the mother house had lost most of its former authority. It is probable that, to all intents and purposes, the priory reverted to a Benedictine house in the fifteenth century. Nor did the double house arrangement survive this conflict; male religious at Amesbury disappear completely after 1400, and at the dissolution (discussed below) Amesbury possessed nuns alone.

One problem relating to the priory cannot be ignored. The publication in 1900 of the results of discoveries made during building work at the abbey mansion in 1860 reopened a heated controversy about the precise location of the abbey church and conventual buildings. The issue cannot be finally resolved until further archaeological investigation takes place, but some attempt may be made at weighing the arguments in the light of knowledge not available in 1900.

The main sources of evidence used in the 1900 arguments were the surviving fabric of the present abbey church, the discovery of tiles, artefacts and the foundations of walls in 1860 on the abbey mansion site, and scattered documentary references. The kingpin of the argument that the present abbey church was the principal priory church rests on a fairly close correspondence (except in the length of the nave) between its measurements and measurements of the priory church taken at the time of the dissolution. It has further been argued that the present abbey church is too large not to have been the priory church; also that the predominantly Early English style of the present church is consistent with building work undertaken soon after the refoundation; and that there is architectural evidence of a cloister on the north side of the nave. For such arguments to carry weight it must be conceded that the discoveries on the mansion site, three hundred metres north of the church, could not have belonged to the convent proper (which was always grouped around the cloister adjacent to the church) but must have been part of an outlying building, the infirmary complex or the prioress' lodgings.

The principal counter-argument lay in examining the accounts of the dissolution, in which, along with most of the conventual buildings, the priory church was ordered to be destroyed, as being deemed superfluous. It is clear that, by 1542, the priory church was in ruins; and yet in the same year a plumber was paid to repair the chancel roof of the parish church, and a parishioner willed to be buried in the church of St. Melore, for which he would provide a number of adornments. Furthermore, the 1860 excavations yielded an object thought to be a holy water stoup (appropriate only to a church), numerous tiles and evidence of molten lead (melting of the lead accompanied the demolition of the church). Indeed the principal room uncovered was conjectured to have been the chapter house, a building which must have been adjacent to the church.

To this list of objections (but a fraction of the many arguments put forward by either side) we would add two observations: firstly, it seems very odd that the priory church should have been thought superfluous if it were also the sole parish church for a town of significant size; and secondly, if the conventual buildings are drawn out in their normal positions, and in accordance with measurements of lead roofs preserved from the accounts of the dissolution, the convent kitchen would have occurred at the north-west corner of the cloister; now we know that the prioress' lodging and associated buildings adjoined the convent kitchen, and further that it was this part of the priory, and this alone, which was retained and subsequently formed the basis of the abbey mansion. If this argument is valid the nave of the priory church must have lain little more than the length of the cloister (about 32 metres) to the south-east of the present abbey mansion. That such a layout existed is substantiated by the observations of William Kemm and his friends, who in June 1870:

> Took a walk in Amesbury park with Mr. Job Edwards, Mr. J. Zillwood and his son Mr. F. Zillwood. The season having been a very dry one caused the foundation of the old abbey and of later walls to show, by the grass being parched. The buildings of the ancient abbey were evidently very extensive, reaching seventy or eighty yards from the present house towards the lodge at Grey Bridge (i.e. the east) . . .

This testimony, if the observations are correct, is quite consistent with the normal monastic pattern, and is a strong argument in favour of the 'two churches' theory.

Excavation currently taking place immediately west of the present church nave may contribute new evidence to the debate. Preliminary findings suggest that the medieval nave did not extend very far beyond its present western limit; if this is the case, it is hard to see how the known measurements of the medieval abbey church can be made to correspond with the present church. It should be emphasised, however, that a great deal more work must be done before the question can be resolved. The following reconstruction is presented as a hypothesis which seems to fit the known evidence.

In 1177 the incoming prioress and her 21 or 24 accompanying nuns occupied the buildings which already existed, probably adjoining the present abbey church on its northern side. By 1186 a new church and conventual buildings had been built to the north of the existing church, near the abbey mansion site, to which the nuns transferred, vacating the original abbey buildings for use by the male religious (who had arrived by 1189). The church which exists today became the prior's church and was also used by the townspeople as their parish church. In the thirteenth century it underwent improvements, including lead for the roof in 1246. This would also explain the rapport which seems to have developed between the prior and the brethren on one side and the parishioners on the other—most clearly seen in the episode of Prior Dawbeney (a local name) narrated above. The prior and his brethren would perhaps have lived in buildings north of the quire which were later incorporated into the former vicarage. After 1400, when the number of male religious in the community was diminished and ultimately disappeared, the present abbey church would have been used solely as the parish church, which it remains today.

Such an interpretation was indeed hinted at in the 1900 controversy, but it was not then realised how significant had been the male element in the community, nor that Amesbury, as a Fontevraldine house, would have been a true double house, possessing two churches and two convents.

Pilgrims and Legends

If landed interests and material possessions contributed to the priory's wealth, there were also spiritual assets. A mania for pilgrimage, rekindled by the murder of Thomas Becket in 1170, brought added prosperity to all religious communities which could claim the relics of a notable saint or martyr. Amesbury as a place of pilgrimage had St. Melor; and because pilgrims were also sightseers, Amesbury could also boast Stonehenge. Legends about both were resurrected and embellished, and later an Arthurian association was strengthened by the claim that Guinevere was buried at Amesbury. The medieval legends, romantic and tendentious, still exist. As historical documents they must be discounted, because their intention was to impress rather then inform. But because they drew pilgrims to Amesbury, were told and re-told, believed and wondered at, and are still believed, they have become a part of Amesbury's history.

In the previous chapter it was suggested that Melor's relics and the legend of his martyrdom arrived at Amesbury after the foundation of the first abbey. His cult was certainly well-established by the time of the refoundation, as William of Malmesbury, writing at the beginning of the twelfth century, believed that Melor was buried at Amesbury. Two hundred years later the bald account of the saint's martyrdom, which had originated in Brittany, had been elaborated at Amesbury and various additions were circulating which seem to have been tailored to explain the changes which took place in 1177. These fables explain how the relics were brought by itinerant priests to Amesbury, where they stuck fast to the high altar, were purchased by the abbess and remained. Later thieves stole the relics and hid them in a nearby cave, until a priest named Godric discovered them and returned them to the church. His efforts were greeted by the martyr himself, who prophesied that the building would collapse and asked that his bones once again be removed. After this was done, the building collapsed. Reading between the lines of these stories it is clear that by 1350 (when they were collected and written down) the relics were no longer to be seen at Amesbury and that the building in which they had lain was destroyed, or perhaps rebuilt. It is tempting to see in these picturesque explanations a shadow of the upheaval which occurred at the refounding in 1177, as well as the excuses of the guide who could no longer show the pilgrims the relics which they had come to venerate.

By the time that the Melor legends had attained their final form in the fourteenth century, Amesbury priory had achieved fame as the sanctuary and resting place of royal ladies, notably Queen Eleanor of Provence, who was buried here in 1291. This repentant sinner was doubtless the model for the Guinevere immortalised by Malory, who in the *Morte d'Arthur* (completed 1469) took the veil at Amesbury and died here before Lancelot, her lover, could gallop from Glastonbury to console her. The association of Guinevere with Amesbury seems to have begun in the fourteenth century and continued until at least 1800, when visitors were still being shown her alleged tomb.

Three hundred years before Malory, however, Arthurian figures were already at large in the neighbourhood. In a curious medley of historical romance, fantasy and genuine folklore Geoffrey of Monmouth, the twelfth century chronicler, sought to explain the mystery of Stonehenge. The principal claim of his account, that Merlin miraculously transported the Giant's Dance from Ireland is well known and has been extensively studied, but certain lesser details shed light on the importance of the monument to the status and attractiveness of Amesbury Abbey as a place of pilgrimage. In particular his claim that the abbey, or 'cloister of Ambrius,' was of even greater antiquity than Stonehenge (which was built to commemorate warriors buried in the cloister) reads like an attempt by the abbey to impress sightseers with its own importance. The burial of slain warriors (460 altogether) perhaps appears in the story to explain the numerous barrows of all kinds dotted around the neighbouring landscape. And the appearance of Ambrosius Aurelianus, a shadowy companion of the British resistance at Stonehenge, is doubtless an echo of an Amesbury legend based on the etymology of 'Ambrosbury'.

Geoffrey's explanations may have satisfied medieval travellers but do not, in general, impress historians. Certain details (such as 'Ambrius') seem to be his invention, others are adaptations of earlier sources not located to Amesbury, still others embody local propaganda; only the notion that Stonehenge was brought from foreign parts (as indeed it was) may represent a genuine tradition, preserved in different forms and in various places, and testifying to the extraordinarily potent curiosity that has always surrounded Amesbury's most precious attraction.

Melor, Guinevere and Merlin continue to haunt Amesbury imaginations. When Amesbury forgets its demi-gods it will have lost something very precious.

The Medieval Town

A town clustered around the gates of a famous monastery was the nearest that medieval Europe came to the nineteenth century industrial town, encircling the factory on which it depended. An abbey was a kind of medieval factory, employing various skills to produce the necessities of daily life. A lease of 1560[1] lists a number of buildings and operations that had been part of the former priory precinct, including: barns, stables, blademills, garners, orchards, dovecots, gardens, ponds, woods, fishing and floodhatches, besides the strictly agricultural concerns. Amesbury men and women doubtless found employment here, whilst others were engaged in the service of individual members of the monastic community. A certain Pontius Florak, for instance, who lived in 1323 at a house in Pouncette Street, Amesbury[2] appears in another document[3] as a bailiff of the nun Mary, daughter of Edward I. Together with two accomplices, also Mary's servants, he had tried to recover possession of a house which Mary owned at Ugford, near Wilton, and his zeal had landed him in Old Sarum gaol.

Quite apart from the prosperity which the abbey as a place of pilgrimage bestowed on the town, therefore, it also provided employment for a number of its inhabitants. In addition it dominated the religious life of the town, which appears to have had no parish church apart from the present abbey church, and this, as we have suggested, was controlled by the priory, at least until 1400, either for the nuns themselves or as the prior's church. It need hardly be said that a medieval town's church was the most important and powerful institution which it possessed.

It may come as a surprise, therefore, in view of the priory's apparent domination of medieval Amesbury, to learn that until quite late in its history the prioress owned no property in the parish other than her own precinct. The old royal manor of Amesbury (or Amesbury Earls as it came to be known) passed through a succession of hands in the five centuries separating the conquest from the dissolution. Lords of the Amesbury manor included members of some of the principal families of England—Lancaster, Despencer, Montagu, Nevill, Clarence— but for much of its history it was in the hands of the earls of Salisbury, and it is to this connection that both Earls Court and Countess Court Farms owe their names. The manor of Amesbury Earls controlled by far the largest proportion of the parish. Gradually, however, from 1286 onwards, the prioress accumulated lands in Amesbury and these had, by the time of the dissolution, been grouped together to form the manor of Amesbury Priors. They mostly lay in West Amesbury. Other parcels of land in Amesbury were at various times distinguished as manors: 'The Conyger' manor, recorded in 1382, is remembered by the name Coneybury Hill in West Amesbury; another West Amesbury manor, known as 'Dawbeneys,' had a protracted existence from the thirteenth to the seventeenth centuries; a house with two mills and a few acres of land in Amesbury is described as the manor of Cantilupe and may, at the time of the dissolution, have become the manor of Souths, although this is conjectural.

Much more detailed study is necessary before a full description of the agricultural and community life of Amesbury in the middle ages can be determined. Here, as elsewhere, the open field system of farming was used, the town being surrounded by enormous fields divided by baulks into furlongs which were themselves divided into long strips, or acres. Originally two, but later three, fields were employed in rotation, to allow a period of fallow. Most households who were not employed by the priory or engaged in a trade would have worked their acres in the fields, at first as villeins, un-free servants of the lord of the manor, whose condition was little better than slavery, but later in the medieval period as free tenants of the lord. A few would have been directly employed by the lord to farm the demesne land of the manor. From the Antrobus Deeds we may glimpse this system at work, especially in the common fields of West Amesbury, which formed the priory lands. A document of 1397[4] refers to three fields—West Field, South Field and East Field—and the first of these, West Field, seems to have survived intact until eighteenth century enclosure. It was bordered by Coneybury Hill on the north and the parish boundary on the south. South Field lay across the river from West Amesbury; by 1612 it was being known as South Ham Field and in the Flitcroft Atlas of 1726 it is divided into Little South Ham Field and Great South Ham Field. East Field does not recur after 1479, but instead two other fields in West Amesbury are mentioned, Middle Field, which lay to the north of Coneybury Hill, and Half Borough Field, which lay to the west of Vespasian's Camp ('borough' presumably refers to the hillfort). Individual tenants farmed acres dotted haphazardly about these fields, so that each had his share of good and bad land. The fields of Amesbury town also figure in the Antrobus Deeds, although less prominently and mostly after the dissolution. Thus we have Barnard Field (1602), in the area of the Boscombe Down complex, Black Cross Field (1612), east of the main road to Salisbury, South Middle Field or South Mill Hill Field (1692, 1612), west of the Salisbury road, Town End Little Field (1613), on the site of Coldharbour and the council estate, and Countess Field (1502) to the north of Amesbury. Other fields also existed on the land later occupied by Earls Court Farm and Ratfyn Farm

In addition to the main concern of farming the arable land a variety of animals was reared. Cattle, jointly owned by the whole community, and sheep manured the arable land in winter or when left fallow, and grazed on the downs and in the meadows in summer. Sheep might be owned either by the lord of the manor, whose flock at Amesbury ran into thousands, or by individual tenant farmers who would pay for a shepherd in common. Amesbury's sheep flock was so large in 1295 that extra labour had to be hired for the shearing. Horses and oxen were bred for work; pigs and rabbits supplemented the meagre diet. Perhaps typical of the Amesbury peasant farmer in the middle ages were John and Christine Balet,

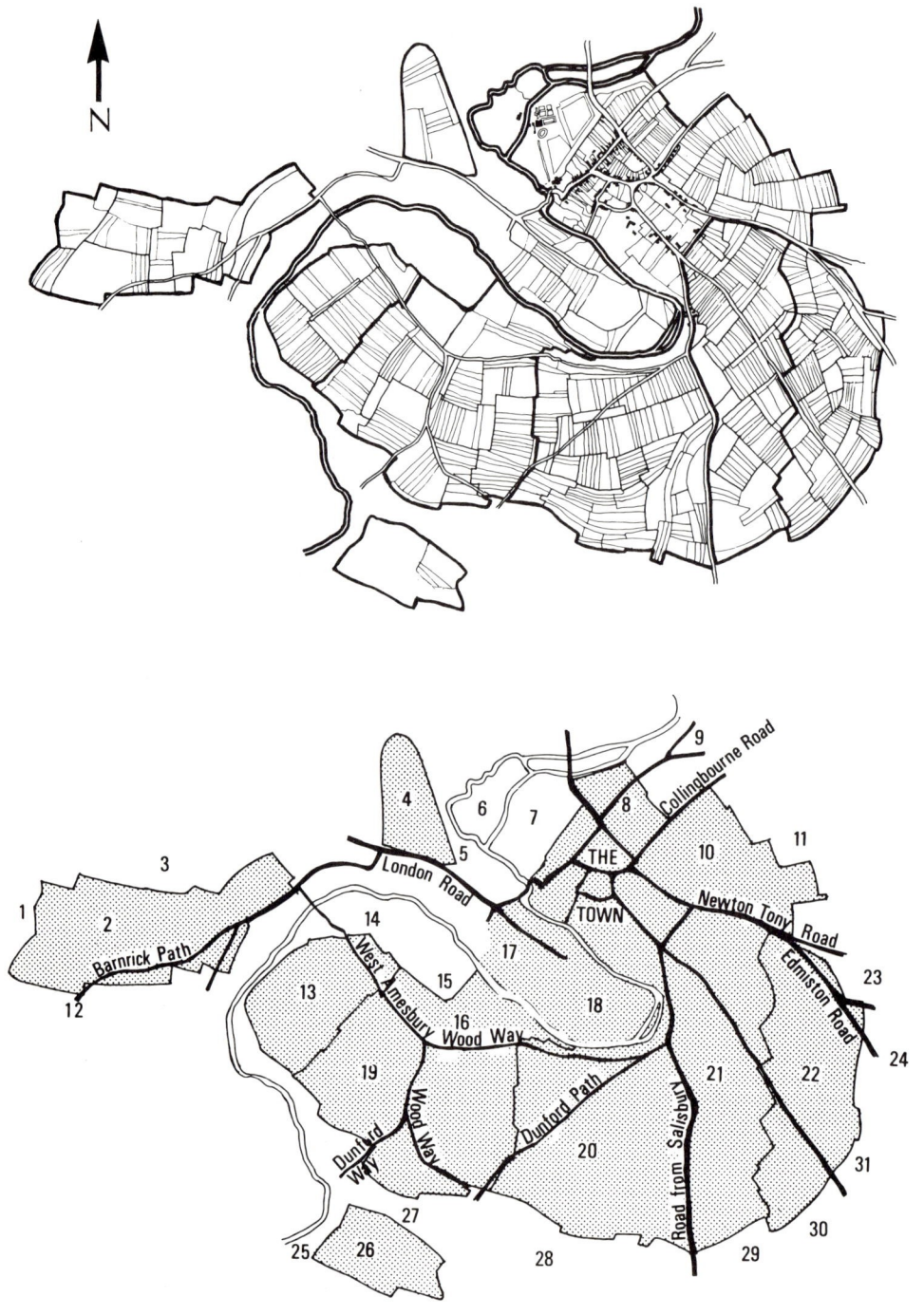

THE COMMON FIELDS OF AMESBURY IN 1726

The two maps opposite show the common fields of Amesbury divided into furlongs and acres (top) and the principal fields, roads and trackways (bottom) as they appear on the 'Book of Mapps' by Henry Flitcroft, commissioned by the third duke of Queensberry in 1726.

1 Abbey Down
2 West Field
3 Middle Field
4 Walls Field
5 Pit Fall Hill
6 Laundry Mead
7 The Demesne
8 Town End Little Field
9 Ratfin Farm
10 Cuckold's Hill Field
11 Earl's Farm Middle Field and Lower Field
12 Normanton Lordship
13 Little South Ham Field
14 Cow Leas
15 South Ham Closes
16 Goose Land Furlong
17 Little Field over the Water
18 Wet and Dry Whitnams
19 Great South Ham Field
20 South Mill Hill Field
21 Bartnett Field
22 Black Cross Field
23 Earl's Farm Upper Field
24 Town Down
25 Pidgeon Hill
26 Woolson Hill Field
27 Woolson Hill Down
28 Lower Down
29 Vinons Farm Down
30 Kickdom Down
31 Black Cross Down

whose farm in 1497 consisted of one messuage (dwelling), half a virgate of land (perhaps about six hectares), two acres (less than one hectare) of meadow, pasture for one horse and five oxen, fifty sheep, two rams and ten pigs.[5]

In its method of agriculture Amesbury was no different from villages throughout the country. As a small town, however, it had attributes not shared by its neighbours. We have seen that it was the eponymous centre of local administration, the hundred, which was in 1334 the second most prosperous hundred in Wiltshire. The lord of its manor derived various benefits from being also the lord of the hundred. It was a judicial centre as well, the venue for hundred courts, in addition to the local manorial courts leet and baron, by which the common fields were managed and wrongdoers taken to task. Most important of all it possessed a weekly market, granted to the priory in 1317 to be held on Saturdays, and annual fairs, of which the most important was held on 6th May, a date associated with St. Melor. This trading function, besides allowing the manor to sell its surplus produce, enabled specialist skills and crafts to develop in the town. According to the Antrobus Deeds a carpenter, baker, washerwoman, fleshmonger, merchant, draper, cobbler, tailor, leatherworker and chandler all existed in medieval or tudor Amesbury.

A number of the streets of medieval Amesbury are known by name. Salisbury Street, first mentioned in 1551,[6] is the only one to bear its present name. High Street was formerly known as Marlborough Street,[7] a name still in use as late as 1816.[8] Frog Lane (now part of Flower Lane) occurs in a document of 1463,[9] and two unidentified streets, Carpenter Street and Pouncette Street, occur as early as 1321 and 1323.[10] The existence of a 'street of carpenters' at so early a date suggests the presence of tradesmen in force even before the market had become established, connected perhaps with building work for the priory. It is clear from the context that Carpenter Street ran roughly north-south, and so it may be an early name for the road which later became Back Lane and is now School Lane. 'Pouncettestret' or 'Pouncestes Strete' seems to refer to Pancet, or Penchet, an old name for Clarendon Forest. The origin of Smithfield Street remains a mystery. It does not occur in the medieval Antrobus Deeds, although it must have existed from an early date. Could it be that it is a corruption of South Ham Field Street, or is the name derived from its proximity to the market?

Archaeology alone can now recover details of the buildings which once lined these medieval streets. We know that there were three inns—the Three Cups in Marlborough Street, the present George (probably fifteenth century although the earliest documentary reference is 1560), and the Swan (perhaps on the site of the present Bell Hotel). We have too a description of a piece of redevelopment in 1474:[11]

> Lease indented for 40 years by Robert Saucer to William Clarke of Great Ambresbur' and Margaret his wife of a tenement with a garden in Marleborghstrete between the tenement of the lessees called "le yatehous" and the tenement of the prioress and convent . . . The lessees covenant to build the tenement anew in manner fit for dwelling in, as in hall, chamber, shop and solar, with all parcloses (partitions), keep them in repair at their own expense and so repaired to leave them.

Estimates of medieval population must be made with very great caution. In the previous chapter we suggested that the population of Amesbury in 1086 may have been about seven hundred. During the next 250 years no figures are available, but it appears that the population of Wiltshire generally grew quite significantly. A tax assessment of 1334 suggests that Amesbury had become a prosperous town. Taking together the assessments for Great Amesbury, Amesbury Priors and West Amesbury, the wealth of Amesbury was exceeded by only six places in Wiltshire—Salisbury, Chippenham, Bremhill, Corsham, Wanborough and Donhead. It would perhaps be reasonable to guess that Amesbury's population had risen, by the year of the Black Death, 1348, to about one thousand. The effect of the Black Death on Amesbury is not known, but at neighbouring Durrington 18 out of 41 holdings had fallen vacant by 1349. A similar casualty rate at Amesbury may be reflected in the poll tax return of 1377, which gives an adjusted figure of about six hundred for the total population. Nonetheless, Amesbury was still more populous than most Wiltshire communities, including boroughs, and was surpassed only by Salisbury, Wilton, Melksham, Mere, Marlborough and Malmesbury.

The Dissolution

The dissolution, by Henry VIII, of every surviving monastery in the land during the decade 1530—1540 is commonly misconceived as a religious act, part and parcel of the reformation of the English church and the estrangement from Rome. In practice it was an attempt to redistribute the ownership of land throughout the country to private magnates at the expense of the largely inactive and spiritually redundant monastic estates. The stark remains of ruined abbeys suggest a brutality in the dissolution which is misleading; in general the process was achieved with due regard for the welfare of the dispossessed inmates, an adherence to the letter of the law and only muted opposition. However, the implications of the disappearance of the abbey for Amesbury after nearly six centuries were enormous and far-reaching; they mark the end of a chapter of the town's history and a new beginning.

Dissolution, at first sporadic and then, from 1536, concentrated on the smaller communities, reached its peak in the years 1538 and 1539, when every monastery, even mighty Glastonbury, found itself under threat of closure. The prioress of Amesbury, Florence Bonnewe, was visited by two commissioners on 29th March 1539, who hoped to take immediate possession of the convent, as they had recently done at Shaftesbury and Wilton and some forty houses altogether. Florence Bonnewe, however, sided with the minority of monastic heads who resisted, whether from a genuine distaste for the proceedings, or merely in order to buy time for her nuns to make suitable arrangements for their welfare. Her refusal to accept a pension and her offer to resign suggest the former. However, by her stand she earned a respite for her house of eight months, until 4th December 1539. By then her resignation had been obtained and a new, more compliant, prioress appointed. This was Joan Darrell, after Florence Bonnewe probably the most senior and respectable member of the convent. She surrendered her house, one of the last monasteries in the country to yield to dissolution, and received a pension, along with the thirty-three nuns still residing at Amesbury. With her surrender the priory of Amesbury was brought to an end.

CHAPTER FOUR: LANDLORD, TENANT, AND LAND

The Squire

To the inhabitants of Amesbury in 1540 it must have seemed as if the end of the world had come. The old order, dominated by the priory, was taken apart stone by stone and carted away by merchants for use elsewhere; Amesbury found itself under the control of a secular lord, Edward Seymour, then Earl of Hertford and later Protector Somerset. In place of the venerable monastery, with its pilgrims and legends, there now arose a gentleman's seat, constructed out of the only parts of the priory deemed worthy of preservation—the hall, buttery, pantry and kitchen. Seymour was more powerful in Amesbury than the prioress had ever been. Not only did he hold the manor of Amesbury Priory, which was granted to him in 1541, but also the other important manor, that of Amesbury Earl's, which the crown had given him in 1536 in preparation for the dissolution. Thus for the first time virtually the whole of Amesbury was under the control of a single owner, and so it remained until the manorial system lost its influence in the last century.

The Seymour family retained the Amesbury manors through successive generations until 1675, in which year John Seymour, fourth duke of Somerset, died without issue. There were, it is true, precarious moments in this long tenure. For a few years in the 1550s the property was confiscated by the crown, and between 1611 and 1615 the rightful owner, Sir William Seymour, was in exile in France. However, there is plenty of evidence that members of the Seymour family spent considerable periods in residence at Amesbury, during which they built the two surviving lodges, Kent House and Diana House, and after 1660, the first purpose-built mansion, the precursor of the present Amesbury Abbey. Whilst it is true that the family was important in the social life of the nation, having produced patrons of the arts and great beauties (for one of whom a rejected lover committed suicide in an Amesbury inn after writing a love song in his own blood), and whilst it is also true that Seymours held some of the highest offices in the land, it must be confessed that, of all the principal owners of Amesbury, they seem to have contributed least to the life of the town.

The estate passed by marriage to the Bruce family, who retained it for some forty years, 1676–1720, before selling it to a prominent statesman, Lord Carleton. Carleton's fondness for avenues is preserved in 'Lord's Walk,' but he cannot have lived to see his lime trees reach maturity, since he died after a mere five years at Amesbury, in 1725. Carleton bequeathed the manors of Amesbury to his nephew Charles, third duke of Queensberry, and Amesbury appears to have embarked on an eventful era under a squire more than usually enlightened to the civic duties which his privileged position ought to entail.

Queensberry and his wife Catherine (or 'Kitty') were forceful characters and influential members of fashionable society. Incurring the wrath of the court over their patronage of the poet John Gay—traditionally held to have written the

Beggar's Opera in the abbey grounds—they defiantly welcomed their ostracism and became the talk of the noble circles in which they moved. During their long association with Amesbury, which ended with the duke's death in 1778, the town underwent changes, some dramatic, some insidious, such as seldom occur in the life of a community. These changes, the disastrous fires of 1745 and 1751, the process of enclosure of the common fields, the inauguration of the turnpike trust and the building of Queensberry bridge, will be discussed in their proper places, but it is important to realise that they all took place within thirty years of each other, and behind each project and improvement may be seen the hand of Queensberry. By egalitarian modern standards the duke's elaborate gardens, fine house and lavish entertainments may suggest shallow generosity to the squalid tenants who surrounded him; but even if stories of Kitty's charity are apocryphal—she apparently furnished her cottagers with specially designed "warm snug chairs of straw"—the third duke of Queensberry and his wife were no worse than many of their contemporaries, and immeasurably better then their successor.

In 1778, when the duke died without surviving issue, the Amesbury estate passed to his cousin, William Douglas, who thereby became the fourth duke of Queensberry. Few kind words have ever been written about 'Old Q,' as he was known, and it is most unlikely that any passed the lips of his Amesbury tenants between his arrival in 1778 and his death in 1810. By all accounts his chief interest in Amesbury lay in the price he might obtain by selling it, and this became, if the turnpike accounts are typical, one of the preoccupations of his life. He was successful in renting the mansion for short periods during his prolonged absences, notably from 1794—1800 to a group of refugee nuns from Louvain, but by the time of his death the fine Webb house had fallen into such disrepair that almost total rebuilding was necessary.

'Old Q' died a bachelor, and the estate was ultimately put up for sale. The buyer, in 1824, was Sir Edmund Antrobus. Members of the Antrobus family have remained lords of the manor to this day. Undoubtedly the squirearchy, as represented by Sir Edmund, continued to be a potent force in local society throughout the nineteenth and into the twentieth century. To commemorate Queen Victoria's coronation, for instance, Sir Edmund and Lady Antrobus provided a meal of roast beef, plum pudding and strong beer for five hundred of Amesbury's labouring population. It was probably the most substantial meal that many of them ever had in their lives. Comparable generosity was shown by later Antrobuses to mark the same queen's diamond jubilee. In the present century we have Antrobus House, Antrobus Road and the Antrobus Arms Hotel to keep alive an otherwise defunct loyalty.

Such have been the landlords of Amesbury, famous and infamous, good and bad. Because they shaped Amesbury's past their history is the history of the town. But the squire was only one out of a thousand inhabitants and his mansion only one out of two hundred dwellings. His tenants also deserve their place in the history of the town.

The Tenants

The ordinary people of Victorian Amesbury are not listed in the directories, and their names are not inscribed on memorials in the abbey church. To all intents and purposes they are forgotten. And yet the biography of any one of them, if it could be written, would be quite as interesting as that of a Queensberry or an Antrobus. Rather than generalise, therefore, about the labouring poor of Amesbury over several centuries, we shall focus on a single year, 1851, the year of a census and, so far as we can tell, a fairly typical year in the life of nineteenth century Amesbury. We shall consider the whole population under this heading of 'tenants,' because, although by no means everybody was the tenant of the squire, Sir Edmund Antrobus, most were, and those artisans, tradesmen and professional people who were not, nonetheless depended on his tenants for their livelihood.

The population of Amesbury in 1851 was 1,172, about one quarter of the present total. Most of the inhabitants lived within three hundred yards of the Market Place. Those who did not dwelt in cottages near one of the farms, West Amesbury, Countess, Ratfyn, or at South Mill. The eighty-three least fortunate members of society existed at the workhouse recently built on South Mill Hill. Repeated fires had changed the face of Amesbury, but the town had expanded hardly at all during the previous 150 years. The people were much the same too. Nearly two-thirds of the population alive in 1851 had been born in Amesbury; only one in ten had come from further afield than south Wiltshire or nearby parts of Hampshire. A mere eighteen inhabitants had not been born in England south of the Thames. Consequently there was a great deal of intermarriage between Amesbury families, so that few of the indigenous population cannot have been related, however distantly, to one another. A further consequence was that certain surnames were extremely common: nearly one fifth of the population was called Truckle, Rattue, Pike, Cooper, Eyres or Mundy. Other local names were Rolfe, Asher, Kilford and Spredbury. It is pleasing to note that descendants of many of these Amesbury families are still prominent in local affairs.

The population in 1851 was a great deal younger than it is today. Fewer than one in twelve had attained the age of sixty, only 32 had reached seventy and a mere four survived into their eighties. There was no reward for the elderly at the end of a hard life. William Pike, aged 72, was still employed as a shepherd, but when you could no longer work you became a pauper, and if you could not depend on the charity of relations, you went to the workhouse. Patience Rushworth, at 88 Amesbury's oldest resident, was fortunate in that she lived with her nephew, a shepherd, and his family; Mary Rawlings, however, a spinster from Enford, 82 years old, could look forward only to a pauper's death in the workhouse where she lived.

At the top of the social scale were the parson, the physicians and the farmers. Fulwar W. Fowle, perpetual curate of Amesbury, lived well. To minister to the needs of himself, his wife, his two unmarried daughters (the elder of independent means) and his eighteen-year-old son (described as a "scholar-at-home") he employed four house-servants, all local girls. Twice during his incumbency (in 1824 and 1859) he applied to extend the parsonage house to accommodate his ample household. The surgeon, George Best Batho, and the general practitioner, Charles Pyle, both employed servants, and the latter seems to have run a small school for young ladies in his house, for whom he employed two governesses. Perhaps the wealthiest of all the upper class residents was Robert Pinckney, who two years earlier had sold his tenancy of West Amesbury farm, and now in his early fifties lived in retirement with his wife and daughter, four servants and a footman, in the house which has become the Antrobus Arms Hotel. Likewise

Joseph Purnell, whose mother had run the George Inn and who had himself farmed the park lands of the abbey, in 1851 was living a comfortable retirement on an annuity with his housekeeper, his butler and a domestic servant. The active farmers, too, could afford large households: Thomas Tanner (Earls Court farm) employed a governess for his four children, a cook, a groom and two servants; Edmund Olding (Ratfyn farm) and Henry Selfe (Countess farm) had three servants apiece; and Ann Long (Red House and Viney's farm) had four; even Michael Rooke, the 29 year old farmer of West Amesbury, employed two house servants for himself and his young wife. Altogether the monied classes of Amesbury provided employment for about sixty domestic servants, nearly all of whom were unmarried women in their teens or twenties.

Inferior to these petty gentlemen were the master craftsmen and businessmen of Amesbury. It was their presence, some thirty in all, with their own premises independent of the squire and their own employees, that marked Amesbury out as a town among the surrounding villages. None of these industries was very large: Joseph Sandell, tailor and glover, had nine employees; Edwin Andrews, carpenter, employed five men and one apprentice; Joseph Olding, miller at South Mill, employed four. Many craftsmen had a single employee or none at all. Some employed only apprentices, and these might lodge with their master; such were Joseph Gane, a blacksmith, and William Eyers, boot and shoe-maker. In other cases the family business was maintained by the late craftsman's widow; thus Elizabeth Cread was a carpenter employing five men, and Mary Turner a blacksmith with three employees. Seventy-three year old Fanny Gilbert was a, "mistress plumber." Those businessmen who prospered might aspire to a domestic servant, but few could afford more than one. Others, such as Joseph Hillary, a tailor, needed to supplement the family's income by whatever wife and daughter could earn as launderesses, sempstresses or glovers.

Relatively few inhabitants, apart from domestic servants, were employed in what today would be called 'service industries.' There were a number of teachers, mostly unmarried schoolmistresses or governesses; there were the toll-gate keepers, the staff of the workhouse, the shopkeepers, the publicans, and James Maggs, the sole police officer. There were also the staff of the Amesbury Abbey estate—gamekeeper, gardeners and grooms. However, these altogether can have amounted to no more than one in twenty of the population.

Beneath the minor professional people and craftsmen were the men and women who worked for them. Usually styled 'journeymen' they seem to have enjoyed a higher standard of living than their counterpart wage-earners who worked in the fields. In several instances two or more journeymen living together could afford a domestic servant; others were able to support large families; still others were lodgers or younger members of a family, for whom an apprenticeship had enabled them to better themselves. Perhaps one twelfth of the population was employed as journeymen or apprentices.

Next in the social order came the largest category of all, those who were, or were dependent upon, farm labourers. The number of labourers employed by the respective farms was as follows: Earls Farm, 71; Countess Farm, 53; Red House Farm, 39; West Amesbury Farm, 29; Ratfyn Farm, 28. All but the last of these farms was owned by Sir Edmund Antrobus, and so the vast majority of labourers worked land which belonged to the squire. Most farm workers boasted no particular skill (to the census enumerator at least), their duties dictated by the seasons and their masters. There were those who specialised, however, a carter, two dairymen and no fewer then fifteen shepherds. Charles Purdue and John Blake, labourer and ploughboy respectively, were the youngest farm workers, a mere eight years apiece. Many wives and daughters also worked in the fields alongside their menfolk. The number of farm labourers was equalled by the number of their dependants, and altogether this social class included four out of every ten of the population. They were the least mobile of all; all but a handful had been born within a morning's walk of Amesbury. Many farm-workers had large families, with six or more surviving children; George Pike and his wife, both aged 38, had eight children, aged between seventeen years and one month, living at home, but the record for the dependants was held by his neighbour, Moses Truckle, who at a mere 33 had accumulated four children, three nieces, one wife, one nephew and one mother-in-law. To offset their more prolific colleagues, however, it should be noted that many labourers were bachelors lodging with families, or were younger members of a household. On average the Amesbury farm labourer's family was not much larger than the average family today.

By 1851 very few children were not receiving formal education for five years or longer. The schools which existed to cater for their needs will be discussed in a later chapter; here it will suffice to comment on the pattern of school attendance. Most boys began school when they were four and continued until they were at least eight, and usually ten; few stayed longer, as they were required to work in the fields, or, if they were clever, they might be apprenticed to a trade. Girls, on the other hand, usually stayed at home until they were six, and then attended school at least until they were ten, and many remained until they were thirteen. Many would then be employed in domestic service for a period before becoming wives and mothers. Exactly two hundred schoolchildren are listed in Amesbury in the 1851 census, with another thirty-five attending the school in the workhouse.

At the bottom of the social scale came the paupers, with no visible means of support. The more fortunate among them, about thirty in Amesbury, retained their freedom and a little of their dignity by remaining in the community, living with relatives or in the cottages where they had spent much of their lives. A few were perhaps able-bodied but idle, but most were incapable of earning their keep through old age or infirmity. When survival became impossible their only recourse was to the workhouse. The catalogue of names of the eighty-three inmates in 1851 reminds us of a side of Victorian life which we might prefer to forget. Here were to be found the elderly whose partners were dead, orphans left to fend for themselves in a cruel world, and, most depressing of all, the infant children of unmarried mothers. Such was Ann Viney, conceived seven years earlier by a nineteen-year old washerwoman, born in the workhouse, and now joined by a brother, three months old but without a name as yet. He, and the three other unnamed workhouse babies, were a far cry from the squire and the vicar, the surgeon and the farmer, though each took his place within the society of Victorian Amesbury.

Agriculture

Until the arrival of service establishments in the twentieth century, agriculture was the mainstay of Amesbury's economy and the principal occupation, as we

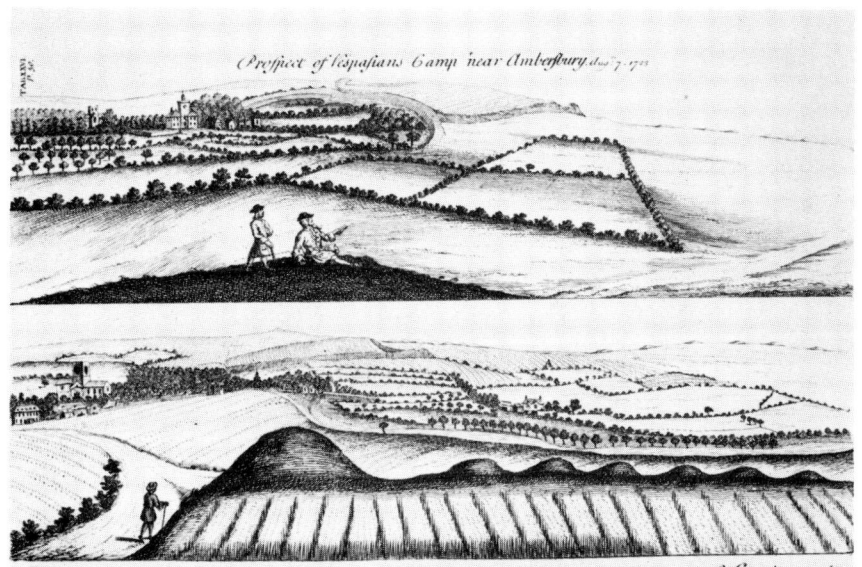

Two engravings by William Stukeley published in 1723. The buildings to the right of the Abbey Mansion in the upper illustration may be remnants of monastic buildings. Large open fields may be seen alongside recently enclosed downland.

have seen, of the largest group of the town's inhabitants. Before about 1750 the pattern of agriculture had changed very little for centuries, the large common fields still being known by their medieval names and still divided into furlongs and acres. This is shown by the magnificent Flitcroft maps of the fields of Amesbury in 1726 and by various surveys. In an extent of 1502, for instance[1], the following fields are mentioned—Countes Fyld, Westfilld, Gret Ambr' Fild, Hawborow Fyld, Suthamme, Lytull Ambresbury Fild, Normanton Fild. Other documents of 1602 and 1612[2] refer to Barnard Field, the Myddle Fielde and Blackecrossefield. Nearly all these names appear on Flitcroft's maps and in a survey of 1742[3]. The names of furlongs and acres endured in similar fashion for centuries until enclosure swept them away in the eighteenth century.

Enclosure, the process whereby the large medieval common fields were divided into smaller, enclosed areas under the control of a single tenant, was not carried out at Amesbury, as in many other places, by Act of Parliament, and so cannot be pinned down to a single date. Since virtually the whole of Amesbury was controlled by one landowner, the duke of Queensberry, he was free to enclose his land piecemeal without legal sanction, and the process may have taken some years to complete. As a result its achievement was perhaps less traumatic to the tenant farmers than in other parishes, where enclosure was imposed at a single date by Act of Parliament. It is clear that the majority of the manor was enclosed between 1742 and 1771; the survey of 1742 records every piece of enclosed land at that date, but with the exceptions of Northams and Southams Closes the only enclosures were gardens, orchards and meads, few larger than one or two acres. By 1771, however[4], most land owned by the manor had been divided between six farms, in order of size, Red House Farm, South Ham Farm, Earls Farm, Countess Court Farm, West Amesbury Farm and Kent House Farm. These six, together with the abbey mansion, controlled 5,105 acres of pasture, meadowland, arable and downland. Fifty years later, in 1824[5] although the total acreage remained about the same, several changes had occurred. The number of farms had been reduced to four, by the incorporation of South Ham into Red House Farm and parts of Kent House (or Park) into Countess and West Amesbury Farms; the proportion of land under cultivation (2670 acres) was now slightly more than half of the total, whereas in 1771 it had been only one third; and the acreage of maiden down, that is downland never cultivated, had been reduced from 2514 to 2056 acres. This pattern is confirmed by an examination of the tithe award for 1841 which shows that nearly all the parish south of Boscombe Road and the river was farmed by William Long of Red House Farm, the land between Boscombe Road and London Road by Thomas Tanner of Earls Farm, West Amesbury and everything south of the present Exeter Road by Robert Pinckney of West Amesbury Farm, and most of the remainder, that is land to the north and east of Stonehenge across Countess Road to the river, by Henry Selfe of Countess Farm. A fifth farmer, Edmund Olding, occupied Ratfyn Farm with five hundred acres north of London Road, but this land did not form part of the Amesbury Manor.

Only the occasional rusting hatchway and derelict watercourses remain of the once complex water-meadow system.

Enclosure was in part responsible for the increased efficiency of agriculture in Amesbury in the nineteenth century, which lasted until the great agricultural depression of the 1870s. A second factor was the gradual introduction of machinery. One such machine, for winnowing corn, invented by a certain John Trowbridge, was apparently named, 'The Amesbury Heaver.' but nothing further appears to be known about this invention. The agricultural labourers, already impoverished by enclosure, did not wish to know about such machines, which posed a further threat to their livelihood, and their concern took the form of a series of incendiary fires at various places in 1830, including two incidents in Amesbury. Mechanisation does not, however, appear to have worsened the labourers' already dismal prospects, as the population of Amesbury increased from 723 in 1811 to 1,065 in 1841 (excluding the inmates of the workhouse) and thence remained steady until the 1890s.

A third, and more important, improvement which took place in the eighteenth and nineteenth centuries concerned the irrigation of water meadows by a system of artificial watercourses controlled by hatches. King's Island Hatches, Bowles Hatches, Ham Hatches and Moor Hatches, all within Amesbury parish, are reminders of this system which, by the controlled flooding of a large area of meadow-land, produced a grass crop earlier in the spring than had hitherto been possible. This enabled more sheep to be kept, which in turn led to more fertile soil for the principal crops of wheat and barley, since the chief value of sheep to the farmer was as a source of manure. This system of farming, involving large flocks of sheep and extensive 'drowning' of watermeadows, persisted until traditional agriculture was ruined by bad harvests and foreign competition towards the end of the last century.

The squire, the tenant and the land, a triangle of exploitation, subservience and hatred. In case we have spoken too glibly about benevolence and improvements, it is fitting that we should close with two passages from the great humanitarian William Cobbett, who saw Amesbury at first hand during a journey down the Avon Valley in 1826:

> If, when a wagon-load of wheat goes off (to market) in the morning, the wagon came back at night loaded with cloth, salt, or something or other, equal in value to the wheat, except what might be necessary to leave with the shopkeeper as his profit; then, indeed, the people might see the wagon go off without tears in their eyes. But now they see it go to carry away, and to bring next to nothing in return.
>
> ... I see it with pleasure that the common people know that they are ill-used and that they cordially, most cordially, hate those who ill treat them.

CHAPTER FIVE: THE TRADING TOWN (1539—1914)

The Clay Pipe Industry

The manufacture of clay pipes in England followed closely upon the introduction of tobacco in about 1570 and continued until the present century. At first concentrated on the large cities, such as London and Bristol, it had spread, by 1600, to most parts of the country, small manufacturers springing up to serve a local area wherever there was a supply of clay suitable for pipe manufacture. Use was very often made of known quarries which had previously been used for the white slip applied to certain medieval pottery. The manufacture of pipes was a skilful and elaborate series of processes, which depended for its success on the careful preparation of the clay, shaping by hand and with a mould, and firing in a kiln for a period of as long as fifteen hours.

In the seventeenth century Amesbury was an important centre for the manufacture of clay pipes, and the quality of its products became famous far beyond the local needs which it supplied. The industry at Amesbury seems to have been confined fairly closely to the seventeenth century; the earliest known example of a 'Fox' pipe (believed to have been made at Amesbury) dates from c.1600, and the latest known maker, Gabriel Bayley, who took over the Gauntlet business in 1698, seems to have disappeared from the town by 1726.

The names of four pipe-makers' firms believed to have been working at Amesbury are recorded although the precise dates of their activity and their whereabouts are uncertain. Edward Fox, whose pipes, embellished with the emblem of a fox on their heels, have been found at Salisbury and Devizes, seems to have been active during the first half of the seventeenth century, although it is not certain that he worked in Amesbury. Robert Smith, a pipemaker at Amesbury in 1664, is known from documentary evidence. Gabriel Bayley, who produced in 1698 a very fine pipe to celebrate his acquisition of the Gauntlet business, does not appear to have survived for long.

The pipe-making industry at Amesbury, however, is primarily associated with the Gauntlet family. The earliest reference to a Gauntlet at Amesbury is 1599 and thence throughout the seventeenth century the name is prominent in local affairs. Two early writers speak favourably of Gauntlet pipes: Aubrey calls them, "the best tobacco pipes in England," and Fuller, "the best for shape and colour," In 1651 the Duke of Bedford ordered a gross of clay pipes for 18/6 from Hugh Gauntlet at the sign of the Swan, Amesbury, and this appears to have been a regular order. Clay pipe-makers regularly used an emblem, stamped on the heel of the pipe, to denote their products, and the Gauntlet family's mark, the palm of a hand, or gauntlet, became such a guarantee of quality that it was taken up and pirated by manufacturers in many parts of the country, especially after the Gauntlet family had ceased trading. A law suit is recorded by the Gauntlets against one of their imitators, which was dismissed on the technicality that the imitator had portrayed the opposite hand. Thus the occurrence of a gauntlet on the heel of a pipe does not necessarily denote that the pipe was a genuine Amesbury product; it is nevertheless a compliment to the high esteem in which Amesbury pipes were held that they should find imitators throughout the country.

The site of the Gauntlets' manufactory is not now known. In the Duke of Bedford's order quoted above it appears that Hugh Gauntlet was connected with the Swan Inn. Aubrey states that the clay for the pipes was brought from Chitterne, and whilst there must be truth in this—Aubrey was personally acquainted with members of the Gauntlet family—it seems likely that there was also a more local supply, which attracted the industry to Amesbury in the first place. According to a local tradition recorded by Kemm and perhaps dating back to 1700 the factory was sited between West Amesbury and Normanton just outside the boundary of the Priory manor at a place known as Wrestler's Gate, and that the pipe-clay was dug on the site. As recently as 1880 a pit at Amesbury was being pointed out as the site of the pipe-clay quarry; its precise location is not recorded, although there is a widespread belief current today that pipes were manufactured in the vicinity of Sloan's garage and Comilla House. Future archaeological discoveries may one day resolve this uncertainty.

Turnpikes and Stagecoaches

Whether through missed opportunities or inhospitable surroundings, Amesbury's career as a roadside town has been less successful than is often imagined. It is true that derelict petrol stations testify to the traffic (now by-passed) of recent years, just as the George Inn and the former New Inn conjure up the busy stagecoaches of the 1830s, but, these two eras apart, the daunting journey across Salisbury Plain seems to have deterred all but the most intrepid of travellers. Amesbury never developed along the Exeter Road in the way that Marlborough (a town of comparable situation and circumstances) developed along the Bath Road.

Roads in general in 1700 were worse than at any time since prehistory. Traffic increased yearly whilst the means of repair, statute labour organised by the parish vestry, remained as half-hearted and inept as ever. Parishes such as Amesbury, which lay on or near main highways, suffered a disproportionate burden compared with isolated neighbouring villages, whose roads were seldom used by any but their own inhabitants. Turnpiking, whereby a group of trustees took over the responsibility for a stretch of road in return for the right to collect tolls from it, came to Wiltshire in 1706, and to Amesbury at the height of the turnpike movement in 1762. By an Act of Parliament of that year the Amesbury Turnpike Trust came into being and, with sixty-two miles of road, became almost the longest of any Wiltshire trust. It controlled the present A303 road from Mullens Pond near Thruxton to Willoughby Hedge above Mere, as well as the road from Stonehenge to Shrewton, Chitterne and Heytesbury, and several shorter sections in the vicinities of Thruxton, Amesbury and Wylye. The purpose of turnpiking local Amesbury roads—Countess Road to the parish boundary, the road from Beacon Hill to Bulford and Larkhill, and from Amesbury to Fittleton via Bulford—seems to have been to prevent travellers from by-passing Amesbury and evading the toll. Tollhouses were set up in Amesbury at the bottom of Stonehenge Road and in Countess Road (surviving), and at Bulford, as well as further afield. Milestones, of which many survive, were set up along the main roads.

The impetus for establishing the trust was provided by the third duke of Queensberry. He became the principal creditor and therefore exercised a controlling interest over its affairs. He also built Queensberry Bridge (in 1775) at his own expense. It was he of course who, as principal owner and landlord, stood to gain most from the trust's success.

The fourth duke of Queensberry inherited the estate, together with the trust's debt of £13,060, in 1778. Over the next thirty years he urged every form of parsimony he could devise on the trust in an unsuccessful attempt to recover the money. The trust made a small annual profit, but it was usually insufficient to pay even a modest interest on the duke's loan, and certainly not enough to reduce the principal.

The first stagecoach used the turnpike for a short period in 1804, and it was greeted with such enthusiasm that some tollgates were farmed (the right to collect tolls was auctioned on an annual basis from 1792) at 50% above the normal figure. This optimism was premature, however, since most Exeter coaches continued to prefer Salisbury until the coaching zenith of the 1830s, when the increase in business made the direct route through Amesbury profitable.

Positive steps to encourage coach traffic were made by the trustees in 1826/7, by widening the road next to the churchyard, and in 1834/5, when they purchased and demolished a house at the bottom of London Road in order to straighten the road. For no more than a decade Amesbury became an important and prosperous coaching town, with nine coaches passing through daily. Most arrived in the middle of the night and all but one used the New Inn (this is not the present New Inn, but the building now occupied by the Post Office and Comilla House). The Exeter coaches—the Defiance, the Subscription, the Telegraph, and the Devonport Mail—all traversed the present A303, but the Swiftsure, between London and Bridgwater, passed through Chitterne.

Amesbury's success in attracting coaches away from Salisbury was spectacular while it lasted. Success encouraged new turnpikes, and two of the last roads in Wiltshire to be turnpiked were those between Old Sarum and Amesbury (1836), and between Amesbury, Rushall and East Kennett (1840). These were not part of the Amesbury Turnpike Trust, but came under the jurisdiction, respectively, of the Swindon, Marlborough and Everleigh Trust, and the Kennet and Amesbury Trust. Too late to profit from the coaching bonanza they have nevertheless left their mark on more recent road development, since the present A345 follows their alignment on most of its course between Salisbury and Rushall.

By 1842 railways had reached Bath and Southampton and the coaching era had died almost overnight. The few coaches which struggled on were only interested now in providing feeder services between important towns, such as Devizes and Salisbury, and the nearest railway station. Amesbury and the A303 were forgotten; The Amesbury Trust's income dropped from £1,181 in 1839 to £370 in 1845. This was not the end of the Amesbury Trust, however; business continued until 1868 when a bondholder took possession of the gates and in 1871 the trust, in common with many others, was wound up by Act of Parliament. Responsibility for roads passed to the newly established Amesbury Highway Board and an auction was held at the George Inn, Amesbury, to sell the trust's tollhouses, gates and effects.

Shopkeepers and Tradesmen

The volume of trade generated by small, inaccessible and largely self-sufficient communities was not great, and it was found to be most convenient to conduct one's business at the weekly market in the local town. Until the lines of communication were improved and the principal of mass production was introduced in the eighteenth century, market trading was the basis of economic life for both the market town and its hinterland. Regular Friday markets had been held at Amesbury since the thirteenth century, but by 1750 the concept of a market was beginning to lose its appeal. The great fire of 1751 probably hastened its demise and by 1809 the Market House was considered redundant and demolished. The broad Market Place, now Salisbury Street, the Market House and the weighing engine have all now vanished, although the lock-up, the symbol of pie-powder justice, remains in the guise of an estate agent's office. By 1830, according to the directory of that year, Amesbury market had become merely nominal.

The fairs, by contrast, of which Amesbury boasted four, lasted longer. These annual events were important to the agricultural community for the large-scale exchange of livestock and produce which took place. Their dates, May 17th, June 22nd, October 6th and the first Wednesday after December 16th, were of great antiquity, associated with the feast days of St Melor and the summer and winter solstices. The May and December fairs seem to have taken place in the town itself, the latter, known as the Amesbury short fair, being the more important in the early nineteenth century, William Kemm remembered: "I have seen when I was very young (i.e. c.1820) the Back Lane, the turning to Bakehouse Lane, and some way along Bakehouse Lane, full of horses at these fairs." The October fair, known as Countess Court Fair, was traditionally held on the downs above Countess, and the June fair was traditionally associated with Stonehenge. The insidious changes of the eighteenth and nineteenth centuries, however, sounded the death knell for the fairs as well as the market, and Amesbury, like the majority of Wiltshire towns, became a place of shopkeepers.

Early directories provide abundant evidence of the shopping habits of our Victorian predecessors. At first, doubtless as a legacy of the market, Amesbury contained a number of quite specialised tradesmen: a soap boiler, brandy merchant, peruke maker and sieve maker (1793); a slopseller, two straw-bonnet makers and a brickmaker (1839). These rubbed shoulders with more predictable tradesmen, who occur consistently throughout the nineteenth century and later: innkeepers, bakers, grocers, drapers, blacksmiths, a saddler, wheelwright and hairdresser, amongst many others. Other trades appear to have declined in importance towards the end of the century, whether because of changing social habits or different channels of supply. No maltsters occur after 1875, although there were two until that year; similarly the trade of beer retailer, which reached its zenith with four traders so described in 1865, had fallen to one by 1885. In the matter of clothing no milliners appear after 1842, the three tailors of 1793 have become two in 1839 and one in 1885, and the four boot and shoe makers who occur regularly from 1793 to 1865 fall to two thereafter. From 1885 there is only one miller instead of two.

Their places were taken by a number of new trades (or old trades under new names) and an increasing number of services. A cattle dealer and a bookseller arrive in 1875, along with the proprietress of a fancy repository. In 1880 a lodging-house keeper occurs and in 1885 a music teacher and a post office. They are joined a decade later by a temperance house proprietor, a district nurse and three laundresses. And once the army was established around Amesbury a plethora of shops and services apppear. The 1911 directory includes a cycle dealer, a solicitor, a coach builder, a bank, tea rooms, an estate agent and a fried fish dealer. Amesbury had arrived in the twentieth century.

Clearly too much reliance should not be placed on directory entries. Errors abound and their quality and thoroughness fluctuate. Taken overall, however, they present a coherent picture of a small rural town in the nineteenth century, adjusting at first to the loss of its market, and then seeing its demand dwindle as the roads to Salisbury and Andover seemed ever more attractive. The coming of the army at the turn of the century provided Amesbury with a much-needed filip, but it seems that the draw of the large shopping centres has once again proved irresistible, and that in this, as in so many other respects, Amesbury has lost most of its former importance.

CHAPTER SIX: SOCIAL CHANGE (1539–1914)

Poverty

Between 1601 and 1834 a parish overseer of the poor existed at Amesbury (as everywhere else) whose function was to levy a rate upon the wage-earning parishioners and use the money thus raised to assist sick and invalid paupers, poor children and the elderly. An important effect of eighteenth-century enclosure and more efficient farming methods was to increase the number of farm labourers for whom there was no work and for whose welfare the parish was responsible. As a small community with limited resources and no endowed almshouses or poorhouse, the problem of poor relief in Amesbury had become critical by the end of the eighteenth century. In 1792 the farmers of Amesbury petitioned their landlord, the fourth duke of Queensberry, for the use of a former inn, the Chopping-Knife, as a poorhouse, with the following explanation:

> The poor of Amesbury are become so very poor and indolent and consequently so burthensome that the farmers are desirous to establish a poorhouse, as by that means, they apprehend, they shall be capable of keeping the real poor more conformable than they now live and oblige the indolent to work and be able to breed up the child in the habit of honesty and industry . . . [1]

Their appeal seems to have fallen on deaf ears, as no more is heard of the proposal, and shortly afterwards a system of supplementing the abominably low wages of farm labourers was adopted and remained until the Poor Law Amendment Act of 1834. During this period living standards continued to decline, however; Cobbett, in 1821, was appalled by the ragged appearance of the Wiltshire peasantry, whose discontent, in Amesbury and elsewhere, manifested itself in riots and incendiary attacks upon farm buildings in 1830.

As a result of the reforms of 1834 Amesbury became the centre of a union of twenty-three neighbouring parishes, which pooled their poor rate resources to build and maintain a workhouse on South Mill Hill in Amesbury. Completed in 1837 it could cater for 150 inmates, with dormitories, sick wards, washhouses, a school, chapel, boardroom, hospital and four yards. Of the twenty-six Wiltshire poor law unions Amesbury was both the largest in terms of the area served, and yet the smallest in terms of population. In 1841 there were 106 persons resident in the workhouse, but ten years later this had dropped to 83.

Workhouses were intended to be austere, a deterrent to the idle poor. Amesbury workhouse was an unpleasant place, damp and dirty, with inadequate food, clothing and supervision. Whether it was worse than those of the neighbouring unions may be disputed. The scandal of the Andover workhouse is well known, and the Amesbury guardians, who administered the workhouse, whilst admitting that the diet was low (per week there were three dinners of pea-soup, two of suet-pudding and two of three ounces of cooked bacon), made the point that it was higher than the standard of living of labourers in the neighbourhood.

The guardians did come in for official criticism, however, which was met by the provision of extra wards in 1873. Thereafter conditions seem gradually to have improved. The workhouse continued in operation until 1930, when the Amesbury Union was dissolved and the property passed to the County Council. It was demolished in 1966/7.

Fires

The most sudden and catastrophic event in the life of any town was a major fire. Combustible building materials and inadequate firefighting equipment, coupled with the widespread use of open fires for many industrial and household processes, spelled disaster for many communities. In Amesbury nine major fires are recorded between 1700 and 1914, the most serious of which, in June 1751, devastated the High Street, causing £10,000 damage and destroying thirty-three houses. For several of the victims this was the second time that their businesses had been reduced to ashes, for a smaller fire had struck the same area six years earlier, claiming one fatality and the lives of a number of horses. Other serious fires occurred in the High Street—Salisbury Street area in 1803, when at least seven houses and other buildings were destroyed, and again in 1899, when the Wesleyan Chapel and temperance hotel were lost.

The humbler dwellings of Coldharbour and Bakehouse Lane (Earls Court Road) were no less vulnerable. Two cottages in Coldharbour were destroyed by fire in 1848 and a conflagration in 1899 claimed a row of eight thatched cottages opposite Earls Court Farmhouse—a drunken navvy employed on building the branch railway line was held responsible for this blaze. A further six buildings in Smithfield Street, including the post office and Ivydene Hotel were burnt down in 1911, an event still deeply implanted on the memories of some older residents.

In the event of a fire it was in everyone's interest to try at all costs to stop it spreading. Amesbury was perhaps luckier than other towns in having had, in the seventeenth century, a vicar, Thomas Holland, who made his name as an inventor of hydraulic engines and pumps. An 'apparatus for extinguishing fires' which he had devised still existed in the church at the time of the mid-nineteenth century alterations; in 1771 it may have been housed in a building in Tanners Lane (Flower Lane) described as 'The Engine House'. The two major fires of 1899, however, found Amesbury unprepared to fight them. In the absence of a local brigade the teams from Salisbury and Netheravon arrived too late to prevent the fires gaining a complete hold. Indeed, in the case of the Bakehouse Lane fire, the alarm was raised by a cyclist who rode to Salisbury at 2 a.m.; it was 5 a.m. before the brigade was on the scene. The disaster led to the establishment of an Amesbury Fire Brigade, which in 1911 was able to respond to the Ivydene fire, "with alacrity."

The devastation caused by fire cannot be overestimated. Some victims were insured, it is true, and it comes as no surprise to find the postmaster in early directories doubling as insurance agent, but for those without insurance the events of an evening could result in a humiliating appeal to charity or a visit to the workhouse.

Religion

We have already hinted that the dissolution of Amesbury Priory was an act of secular, rather than spiritual, importance to the town. Little is known about the impact of the reformation on the spiritual life of Amesbury, although a mood of apathy and submission prevailed in Wiltshire generally. Certainly no incumbent of the town risked his neck by opposition to whichever creed was imposed upon him. It is tempting to surmise from the surviving records that the established church in Amesbury, as elsewhere, has never since the reformation attracted any great enthusiasm in the breasts of the parishioners. In 1662, for instance, the forlorn churchwardens reported to the bishop that the church and chancel, as well as some seats in the church, "are something out of repair," and further:

There are many that absent themselves from sermons. There are many that refuse to have their children baptized, or themselves to receive the communion. There are many that refuse to come to church to give thanks to God for their safe deliverance. There are many that refuse to pay their duty for Easter offerings to our minister.

A century later the position seems to have been little better. The vicar in 1783 replied that, "four or five and twenty is the usual number (of communicants);" the population of the parish was then probably 600—700. In Victorian Amesbury, however, when churchgoing was more commonplace, the number of communicants was about seventy in 1864, and the congregation much larger, and increasing. The vicar could nevertheless report in 1870, "Great indifference to religious duties in some of the higher class, and great immorality in the lower. But I do not know that these such impediments exist here to a greater extent than in other parishes severally."

Two incumbents of Amesbury deserve mention. Thomas Holland, vicar after the commonwealth, was described by a contemporary engineer as a genius, on account of his inventions. Apart from designing a pump which operated the fountain at Wilton House, he installed an engine to supply water to the hill-top town of Shaftesbury. We have already mentioned the fire engine which he designed for his parishioners. Fulwar W Fowle, by contrast, was one of those nineteenth century churchmen whose life work was spent ministering to a single parish. When he died in 1876 he had been vicar of Amesbury for fifty-nine years, and had, as he himself pointed out in a sermon a few years before his death, conducted more burials than the entire population of the parish when he arrived. During his incumbency he was involved in many of the developments which took place in the town in the nineteenth century, as well as presiding over the restoration of the church and considerable improvements to his vicarage.

Besides apathy the established church had to contend with dissent. One of the earliest and most vigorous nonconformist congregations in Wiltshire was active in the Amesbury area before the Toleration Act of 1689. Its leading light was John Rede, a magistrate of the anabaptist persuasion, who lived at Birdlimes Farm, Porton. His inaugural meeting in 1655 attracted over one hundred sympathisers from the surrounding villages, and soon meetings were being held in various places, including the house of Thomas Long at West Amesbury, which in 1669 attracted a congregation of about thirty, and was still active in 1683. The initial enthusiasm seems to have died with the Toleration Act, since no dissenting congregation is listed in an early eighteenth-century survey, and only one building was registered for protestant dissenters' worship at that time (the house of Thomas Cook in 1719).

Dissent returned to Amesbury in the person of John Wesley, who visited the town twice, in 1779 and 1785. After the latter visit he noted in his journal, "I visited the little flock at Amesbury, humble, simple, and much devoted to God." Wesley made a profound impression on the town, reawakening an interest in religion, which resulted in a number of independant, and later methodist, congregations springing up in private houses in Amesbury, Ratfyn and West Amesbury. Even a barn was used. The first mention of a methodist chapel occurs in 1816, and this was relicensed in 1838. It is probably the one which stood on the site of the present chapel in High Street, which was destroyed by fire in 1899. Writing with disdain of this congregation in 1867, Fulwar Fowle commented, "among the lower orders, many who are not dissenters, go with itching ears to hear the sermon." After the disaster of 1899 the community rallied to such an extent that the present building was completed and opened within twelve months of the fire.

Until recently catholicism seems to have played no part in the post-reformation history of Amesbury. The only exception occurred between 1794 and 1800, when the abbey mansion was rented to refugee canonesses from Louvain. They deserve mention, if only for the death of Sister Monica, one of their number, which by a remarkable coincidence occurred while they were celebrating mass on St Monica's day, 1797.

Education

Few ordinary children before the nineteenth century were given any formal education. The lucky ones owed what schooling they received to charitable foundations set up to employ a schoolmaster or mistress from the proceeds of the deceased benefactor's estate. John Rose (allegedly the first man to grow a pineapple in England) in 1677, and Henry Spratt, in 1708, established schools in Amesbury in this fashion, the former for twenty children aged 9—15, the latter for thirty children aged 4—9. Rose's school was originally held in the south transept of the parish church, possibly succeeding an earlier school in the same place; in 1807, after many years of teaching in the schoolmaster's house, it was transferred to the former Jockey Inn in High Street, known to this day as the Old Grammar School. One of its earliest and most distinguished pupils may have been Joseph Addison, born at nearby Milston. Spratt's School never owned premises, the teaching being carried on in the schoolmistress's house. Reading and the catechism were the pupils' first concerns, and until these were mastered they could not pass from Spratt's to Rose's school, where they would learn English grammar, arithmetic, fair writing, cyphering and casting of accounts.

In the nineteenth century the range of education available to Amesbury children was greatly expanded. The two charity schools continued throughout the century, and the trustees of Rose's charity, having accrued a surplus, began a preparatory school in 1819, which continued, under the direction of the Misses Sandell in their own house until the 1840s. From 1821 until its demise in 1896 Spratt's school was run by female members of the Zillwood (or Selwood) family, while Rose's school plodded on under the tuition of two notable masters, William Cox, 1801—1849 and Edward Flower, 1871—1899. A host of new schools also sprang up. A Lancasterian school (based on the monitoring theories of the educationalist Joseph Lancaster) had been established by 1830 and this became, by 1839, the National School, the largest school in Victorian Amesbury, providing an elementary education to as many as one hundred pupils. This school was managed by the Antrobus family in premises of their own, and by 1855 they had augmented it by the provision of an infants' school. This continued under a succession of spinster mistresses until the turn of the century. Besides these more or less permanent institutions a succession of temporary schoolteachers pass through the directories catering for the higher social strata: Miss Caroline Browne, whose day-school (1842) became a boarding school (1855–1865) and who died at an advanced age in 1881; Mr John Zillwood, related to the mistresses of Spratt's school, who ran a day school between 1855 and 1875; and the Rev Arthur Meyrick, who operated, "a preparatory school for young gentlemen," at Wyndersham House (Fairholme) from 1875–1880. Taking all these establishments together it seems likely that in mid-Victorian Amesbury upwards of two hundred children were receiving schooling in Amesbury, and this figure, estimated from directories, tallies extremely well with the 1851 census return discussed in chapter four.

Besides the schooling of young children two opportunities existed for older pupils. A charity established in 1725 by Richard Harrison offered apprenticeships for up to five former pupils of the charity schools. By the end of the nineteenth century awards under this bequest had become sporadic, and the last apprenticeship was awarded in 1897. Rather more successful was an adult evening school, begun in 1859 and conducted by Mr Merchant, the postmaster, at the Wesleyan chapel, which continued with enthusiasm and a government grant until at least 1870.

Towards the end of the Victorian era state supervision of education increased. A School Attendance Committee for the Amesbury Union was established in the 1880s with two attendance officers. By 1900 both Rose's and Spratt's school buildings were considered defective and the National School premises had been condemned by the Education Department as unsatisfactory. Spratt's was in any case moribund and the headmaster of Rose's, Edward Flower, had intimated his wish to retire (in 1911 he is described as a bee-keeper). Negotiations took place in 1900 between Sir Edmund Antrobus, Wiltshire County Council and the trustees of the various charities with the result that, on land in Back Lane (School Lane) presented by Sir Edmund, a new school was erected at a cost of nearly £4,000, which sum was raised from the proceeds of selling the property of Rose's and Spratt's charities. Harrison's apprenticing charity was also included in the scheme, the produce of its assets being used to provide scholarships to the school. The school provided places for 137 boys and girls and 58 infants, slightly less than our estimate of the total attendance of the various schools some thirty years earlier.

Into the Twentieth Century

In the course of four thousand years Amesbury has undergone long periods of relative stability punctuated by occasional upheavals. The founding of the first abbey and the dissolution of the second were two such upheavals, events which lifted Amesbury out of its doldrums and pointed it in a new direction. A third was the agricultural revolution of the mid-eighteenth century. The fourth, and most recent, occurred during the years 1895–1902, and marks a convenient place for this historical essay to end. The history of Amesbury in the twentieth century is best illustrated by describing what survives today, and this the second part of our book sets out to do.

The seeds of Amesbury's latest revolution were sown in 1872, in which year large scale army manoeuvres took place on Salisbury Plain, centred on Beacon Hill and the site of Bulford Camp. Ten years later the plain came under attack from a different direction, the business interest of the London and South Western Railway, who proposed a railway line from Grately via Amesbury and Shrewton to Westbury. A lull followed, until in 1897 both camps made a move. The army, for its part, purchased 750 acres in Bulford parish; the railway tycoons proposed to build a line up the Avon valley from Salisbury via Amesbury and Stonehenge to Pewsey. These two interests conflicted, because the railway would have made a nonsense of the army's plans to use the Avon as a practice area for river-crossings under enemy attack. The army won, the railway scheme was dropped, and a total of 42,000 acres of Salisbury Plain were, by 1902, in the ownership of the War Department. Meanwhile an enormous show of military strength had taken place at Boscombe Down, in the form of a grand review of 50,000 troops attended by 80,000 spectators. As army camps sprang up on the downs all around Amesbury it became clear that the town would take on a new role, providing services and communications to the transient hordes of soldiers and their families. It was clear, too, that to fulfil this function, Amesbury must become more accessible to the outside world. Hence the railway reappeared. On 2nd June 1902 the first train arrived at Amesbury along a new line from Grately and Newton Tony. The line was later extended to Bulford Camp, and branches were made to serve Larkhill, Rollestone, Stonehenge and Lake Down (Druid's Lodge) Camps.

The railway has gone now, its function usurped by road transport. But communications, along with the ever present army and air force establishments, are still the mainstay of Amesbury's economy. We have come a long way from the builders of Stonehenge, the royal nuns, the peasant farmers and the workhouse. The present is ephemeral. Our future will be the better for the interest we take in our colleagues, those generations of men and women who have watched the Avon wind its course timelessly through our little town.

AMESBURY : A DESCRIPTION

Z
Porton Rd
A303T
James Rd
Holders Rd
The Drove
Antrobus Rd
Boscombe Rd
LONDON ROAD
Kitchener Rd
Cold Harbour
Earls Court Rd
SALISBURY ROAD
Cent
Sals St
High St
Church St
Flower Ln
RIVER AVON
COUNTESS ROAD
STONEHENGE ROAD
WEST AMESBURY
BATTLE OF THE NILE TREE CLUMPS
THE AVENUE
km 0
½
1
miles 0
½
footpaths
1
2
3
4
5
6
7
8
9
10
11
12
13
14
15
16
17
18
19
20
21
22
23
24
25
26
27
28
29
30
31
32
33
34
35
36
37
38

CHAPTER SEVEN: INTRODUCTION

The village today still sits quietly in its river valley waiting patiently to receive the passing traveller. Lying in the Avon valley it remains largely out of sight, but fortunately today superior sign-posting points the way and our traveller, unlike yesteryear, does not have to wander across a hostile plain, at risk from robbers, cut-throats and rutted trackways. Development boundaries have been pushed way beyond those of the original groups of dwellings built to serve the needs of miller, farmer, church and lord, and are beginning to creep up the slopes surrounding the village to the high ground beyond.

A GENERAL MAP OF AMESBURY

A general map of the town area showing features referred to in the text.

- - - - - - - footpaths

1 Stonehenge
2 Full Moon Clump
3 New King Barrows
4 Old King Barrows
5 Seven Barrows area
6 Half Moon Clump
7 The Cuckoo Stone
8 Crop markings of early farm settlement
9 Woodhenge
10 Crop markings
11 Long barrow
12 Totterdown
13 Route of former railway, now public path
14 Route of former railway
15 Toll-house
16 Countess Farm
17 Ratfyn Farm
18 Vespasian's Camp
19 The Abbey Mansion
20 Graybridge
21 Lords Walk
22 Former railway station
23 Folly Bottom
24 West Amesbury House
25 Parish Church of St Mary & St Melor
26 Site of former toll-house
27 Queensberry Bridge (otherwise Great Bridge)
28 Almanaze Path
29 Viney's Farm House
30 Ham Hatches
31 Wittenham Footpath
32 Site of former workhouse
33 Toll-house
34 The Durnford Path
35 South Mill
36 The Lynchets
37 Ditch and Pit Alignment
38 Enclosure

The approach roads are lined with an ever thickening ribbon of houses, primarily private developments. Local Authority housing is established in a solid quadrant from north-east around to south-east. Such industry that is permitted to exist here highlights the eastern approach while, to the north, west and south, the farming widely practised here has largely maintained a green belt.

With the exception of the adjacent Boscombe Down airfield and its complex of hangars, buildings and houses positioned to meet the urgent demands of war and aircraft rather than the desires of the environmentalist, development around Amesbury has so far been managed with minimal intrusion into the surrounding countryside. There are signs that this policy which has so far been pursued successfully, if unconsciously, is about to change and that Amesbury may evolve into another urban sprawl across the downland. The traditional approach has not been without its problems though, having produced some fairly high density housing estates within the natural confines, with the result that the village today is but a pale shadow of its former self.

Amesbury lies approximately in the middle of its parish. The approach is made through a landscape of field boundaries that still reflects the reorganisation brought about by enclosure during the 18th century. This pattern is itself disappearing, as the demand for more spacious fields is met in the quest for ever increasing efficiency in farming.

The parish boundary coincides fairly well with such evidence of the earlier manorial boundaries that exists, allowing for the areas that have, more recently, been added or subtracted. Perhaps this similarity gives a hint of common origin.

Evidence of the manorial boundaries is scarce. That which remains results largely from the use of man-made and topographical features. An early road marking the division between adjoining manors became the later London Road, or A303, to the east of the village; the river, from the Woodhenge area downstream to Ratfyn and similarly upstream from Normanton through West Amesbury; the line between the various tumuli on the surrounding downland and the route followed by the various streets in the village. All these features were used, as we see in an extract from the perambulation of 1639 of the Earldom manor:

> ... turning south east between the said Earl's Fields and Ratfield Down to a ball or bound standing upon the top of a great Ditch ... as the said ditch leadeth by one ball between Porton Down on the S.E. and the said Hogg fflock down to the next bound ... N.E. up the river to West Amesbury and so to the several fishing of Sir Lawrence Washington lately called Mr Dawbney's mill-pond ... from the said ash down the middle of the river and so taking in King's Island which is within this boundary and thence down by the same river of Avon to a stone which lieth in the middle of the river ...

The remains of early ditch and bank features, often used to mark boundaries from Saxon times, are visible on the downs to the south of the village, crossing the now metalled track to Durnford. Even this rare feature, though scheduled as an ancient monument has, with other similar features, suffered the onslaught of the plough. So is our history lost. Unfortunately the economics of modern farming, even when properly carried out, do not leave much time for the niceties of history. The subject rarely attracts the sympathy of the average farmer.

An earlier archaeological feature, a pit alignment and ditch rare to this region, is also thought to delineate a territorial boundary and runs in a north-south direction to the west of South Mill Hill. This feature had disappeared without trace until 1976 when the unusually dry summer caused it to show as a crop mark. Other settlement and farming features of the Romano-British period were also brought to light in the same area and to the west and north of the village. As we have seen earlier, the approaches to Amesbury have evolved around the cardinal points by the existence of the ancient east-west trade route and the north-south river valley route which, at their intersection, provide an ideal and sheltered site for the village in the flat and fertile river plain. In earlier years our weary traveller, finding Salisbury Plain not the most hospitable of places, must have searched eagerly for signs of the village before proceeding into the depths of uncharted England.

One of the many previously unknown archaeological features that came to light during the 1976 drought was this rare pit alignment and ditch. Running southwards from Southmill Woods it is thought to represent various phases in a territorial boundary of the Iron Age period, and is probably associated with the extensive settlement known to exist in this area.

Improvements to the A345 at South Mill Hill to the south of Amesbury neatly bisected this pre-medieval enclosure, or penning, that remained undiscovered during the roadworks.

For many years associated with Stonehenge, the normally invisible 'avenue' of twin parallel banks to the north-west of the town can clearly be seen here running through the Battle of the Nile tree clumps as it turns south-east towards West Amesbury.

At the north entrance to the town, in the field adjoining the south edge of Woodhenge, the 1976 drought conditions exposed evidence of this farm settlement from the Bronze Age period. In the background is a barrow alignment.

    The evolution of the road system to today's standard has, of course, been a long and far from steady process. The routes, determined largely by the local topography and seasons, giving us highways for the winter over firmer ground and summer ways following the flatter river courses, depended largely on whether the ground was passable and would meander and vary as hooves and wheels made a particular portion too deeply rutted and impassable. The deep grooving that often resulted can still be seen to the east of Amesbury where the road swings over Beacon Hill, before dropping down to Folly Bottom. Similarly, recent excavations to the south of the village revealed medieval wheel tracks well away from the present adjacent trackway. As agricultural requirements increased, bringing the larger and more well defined field systems, the meandering routes became more and more contained within the narrow confines characteristic of today's road system, bringing of course the inevitable need for improved surfacing. We enter Amesbury today along the results of this almost timeless evolutionary process.

"Spot of trouble with the road Guv?" Pot-holes or a re-surfacing job during the 1920's would bring out this team of stalwarts, to keep the roads in repair.

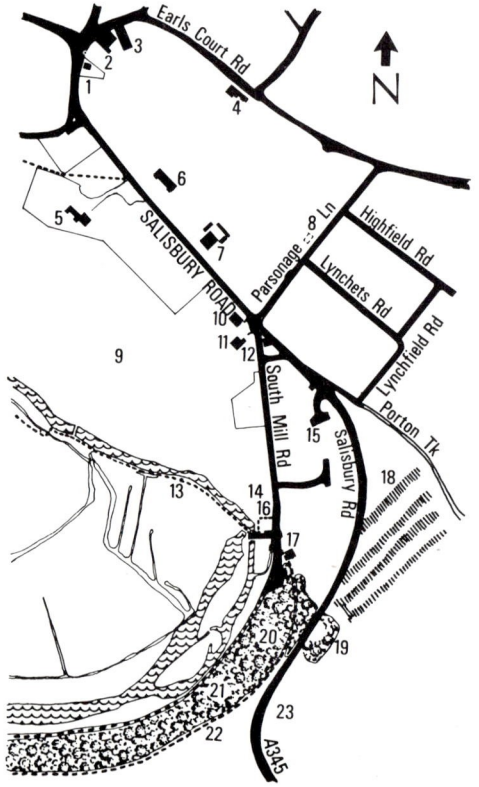

1 The Pound
2 Co-operative Store. Former site of Ivydene
3 Cinema
4 Earls Court Farm House
5 Vineys Farm House
6 Antrobus House
7 Red House
8 Site of former Parsonage Barn
9 Water meadows
10 Police Station
11 Buckland Court
12 Toll-house
13 Wittenham Path
14 South Mill Green
15 Avonstoke Close. Site of former workhouse
16 South Mill
17 South Mill Cottage
18 Lynchets
19 Chalk Pit
20 South Mill wood
21 Durnford track, former Wood-way
22 Durnford track
23 South Mill Hill, formerly Lime Kiln Hill and Workhouse Hill

CHAPTER EIGHT: THE APPROACHES TO THE VILLAGE

South

To arrive at Amesbury from the south today is by two primary routes and a minor one. Of the former, one uses the river valley from Salisbury through the Woodfords, Lake and Wilsford, entering the village via West Amesbury. The other major entry that will be the principal subject here, uses the high ground and takes the form of the present A345 from Salisbury. The line of the present road dates from 1836. Prior to this one would have left Salisbury on the old Roman road, later the Marlborough Coach Road and branch northwards to Amesbury at the five mile post which is the Winterbourne Gunner turning today.

At Southmill the former road from Salisbury winds its way down the hill past the house, to meet with the Durnford track on the way to Amesbury.

The 19th century toll-house at the top of Southmill Road was designed to serve traffic on the old road to the right and the new turnpike at the left.

South Mill Hill   One entered the southern part of the village at Lime Kiln Hill which was also the junction with the Durnford and West Amesbury trackways. The road descended steeply towards Townsend Mill, our present South Mill, the road still being visible today and used as a public right of way, with the bank and hedge—laid for years in the traditional manner—still being discernible. The present road that curves round by the Lynchets was not constructed until the turnpike came into existence, the new route taking it to the east of the workhouse, part of which protruded into the road causing not a little worry to the Board of Guardians which decided not to consult the turnpike commissioners on the matter lest they had to demolish the offending buildings.

Returning to the earlier road at South Mill, the first habitation that the weary 18th-century traveller would meet was the cottage known today as South Mill cottage, thought to have been the "Blue Lion" Inn. At the base of the hill, at the mill, the alternative route to Durnford and the Woodford valley joined the Salisbury road, at South Mill green. Both merged and proceeded north-west along the present South Mill Lane which then extended into the village instead of becoming, as at present, the Salisbury Road once past the 19th century tollhouse. Up to the 19th century, the road ran through the common fields, orchards and closes, a much more open environment than at present. It was, from appearance on the map, the more prosperous farming and residential part of the village. Certainly this area did not seem to possess the numbers of humble dwellings found elsewhere. The common fields immediately to the north of the mill, between South Mill Road and the river, were still used as cricket field, fair-ground and recreation area well into the first quarter of the 20th century. Until 1967 the two principal buildings to be seen at South Mill were the mill itself and the workhouse. The mill still stands, but the workhouse has been replaced by Avonstoke Close, a group of town houses built on the same site. Although no longer with us, the workhouse merits a little consideration here, such was its social impact during its time.

The southerly approach to Amesbury viewed from South Mill Hill at the turn of the century. The workhouse is in the foreground.

A similar view in the early 1930's. Council housing has appeared and already many of the prominent trees have been felled.

The present scene: the workhouse and adjacent farm buildings have gone, replaced by a residential area and police station.

The Workhouse   As we have seen elsewhere, by the 19th century a very real need existed to cater for increasing numbers of poor persons, by providing material or financial aid.

Whilst the abbey had existed it had, if it followed normal practice, tended to the needs of the pauper element, providing such clothing, food and tuition as it was able. Support of the poor later became the duty of the parish and all were returned to it if reduced to pauperism elsewhere. All this, of course, presupposes that a person was able to leave the parish or manor in the first place, for to do so a licence from the lord was required. During the Elizabethan period a poor relief system was set up which continued with varying success until the 19th century, when the might of the Victorian legislative mind was brought to bear on the subject, with the passing of the Poor Law Amendment Act in 1834.

The immediate result of the Act as far as Amesbury was concerned was for the parish to be grouped with others into the administrative unit known as the Union, and a workhouse built for the union on the southern edge of the village. The workhouse was completed and a going concern by 1838. Designed by W. B. Moffatt, a friend and business partner of Sir George Gilbert Scott, it took the established form of three parallel sets of buildings used as wards, dormitories, kitchens, laundries, chapel and boardroom joined at right-angles through their centre by administrative blocks with storerooms, larders, staff quarters and the "usual offices". A central tower affording a good view of the various wings and yards was also used as offices and accommodation. Pigsties, stables, mortuary and various other outhouses were situated around the periphery and a large garden was cultivated to the south. The complexities of the Victorian administrative system caused certain initial difficulties, with Returning Officers complaining that they were unable to complete the various forms and paperwork. The system of supply by competitive tendering also met with opposition from local traders who were not chosen, one in particular complaining that, "Tory tenders (were) being accepted whither cheapest, dearest best or worst . . . "

Poor law relief was run much in accordance with the Victorian concept of making it a socially unacceptable, degrading and unattractive prospect. Men and women were segregated. Families, if admitted, were split up, perhaps not seeing each other again but certainly not being allowed to mix together. The workhouse was a thing to dread and to be avoided if possible at all costs because once inside one rarely emerged on a permanent basis under one's own motivation! As the name of the institution implies, inmates were given work to do to retain their concept of usefulness. Men would pick oakum, grind bones for glue or tend the gardens and livestock. Women would attend to the laundry and cooking; children were given an elementary education before being sent to labour on local farms.

In return the inmates were housed and fed but enjoyed a very rudimentary existence. Their diet received continual criticism and was poor by our present standards but considered quite adequate by the Poor Law Commissioners not so much for its nutritional value but because it was better than that which was available to the average labourer. Living conditions were poor and received their fair share of attention — the yards were muddy, the sanitation poor, with the "soil remaining in the privies . . . " Children, who at various times numbered up to 40, had to be of a hardy breed.

Medical assistance often left much to desire. In January 1840 burst water pipes caused excessive dampness in the girls' bedrooms. The workhouse master put a charcoal brazier in the room to dry them out, removing it 15 minutes before bed-time, putting it downstairs. The bedroom windows were shut tight against the cold night air and the bedroom door left open. Thirty minutes later a girl entering the bedroom found the occupants being violently sick in bed. The master was called and found them "almost in a state of insensibility". He opened the windows and tried to revive the children by using a bucket of cold water. This apparently had little success so he dipped them in a bath of lukewarm water . . . "most providentially they all recovered"; remember, it was January and a particularly hard winter!

The workhouse master did not always appear in such a helpful or benevolent role. On one occasion he was accused of accelerating the death of a boy inmate who was ill and confined to bed. It was alleged that the boy's condition did not impress the master, who pulled him from the bed by leg and arm and threw him across the room, then picking him up and throwing him back onto the bed during which he hit and wounded his head on the stone wall. The master protested his innocence, in this case rightly, as the culprit was later found to be the schoolmaster, a man subsequently described as utterly unfit for the situation in which he was placed. This particular workhouse master was, however, later found to be guilty of beating boys with a rope's end and so he was not entirely without fault. Mind you, his youthful charges may well have driven him to desperation!

Other sad tales include allegations that an inmate with putrefying maggot-ridden wounds was allowed to lie and die of dropsy in a room occupied by healthy men and that the guardians refused to accept into the workhouse a woman "apparently at the last stage of existence." Transporting lunatics to Devizes must have been a hazardous business, with reports of the patients arriving variously with broken limbs, bound and drunk!

With this sort of atmosphere prevailing it is no wonder that fighting is reported among the inmates and that escape attempts were made by whole families, whilst others preferred to take their chance in the colonies. In spite of its shortcomings, the 19th-century poor relief system was a very important social development. The workhouse continued to house various inmates up to the 1950's. It was known also as 'the spike', from the method of filing the meal or relief tickets for the itinerant visitor who, with his distrust for authority, would hide his few belongings in a convenient hole in the bank along the Salisbury Road. It is perhaps sad to note that now the workhouse is gone, demolished in 1967, no place or road names commemorate its existence. Presumably the enlightened few who decide the content of such labels still feel a corporate guilt, generated from the currently unacceptable standards set by their forerunners. Let us quickly forget . . . !

South Mill At the bottom, or southern end, of South Mill Road lies the former mill itself, the focal point of several tracks from nearby villages.

This mill is the last remaining evidence of a trade practised here since before the Domesday period. The present structure is, however, a 19th century rebuilding of an older building. An earlier era is suggested by the stonework in the adjacent mill-leet to the north, which displays more of the green sandstone from the demolished abbey. The mill was certainly in full swing during the early 17th century, when described as containing two water-corn mills; it would have been one of two such establishments at that time, the other being situated by the present gate to the abbey, next to the church. Milling activities had finished by the latter part of the 19th century and, during the early part of this century, the building was purchased by one "Bungy" Woods, presumably as a dwelling and trading premises. Mr Woods, also known as "Beaver" due to his long white beard, was a master builder from Portsmouth. Whilst here, he acquired possession of the common fields that lay immediately to the north-east, from the mill along the river edge to Stonehenge Road, and started a gravel-pit and an ill-fated laundry along the edge of the Wittenham Path. The laundry, although built, came to naught through Mr Woods' scant regard for the planning requirements of local government. He did leave his mark, however, in the shape of the eastern-style bungalows that he built of reinforced concrete, in the London Road and in Church Lane. Remains of the gravel-pit workings are just visible still, with one remaining truck from the narrow-gauge railway. The foundations of the laundry can also just be depicted.

Having exhausted the potential of the area, Bungy withdrew from the scene as quickly as he had arrived. The mill however, with the arrival of electricity embraced this new technology, using it to continue the good service rendered to the community for so long.

South Mill, formerly Town End Mill.

Amesbury Electric Light Company   Electricity was first provided in 1922, with the formation of the Amesbury Electric Light Company which housed itself in the south mill which it purchased from Bungy Woods for around £1200. An office and showroom was set up in the High Street at Chimes House, now the hairdressers establishment, and the Company set about providing an initial supply of direct current from its Hay-Marion water turbine generator.

The first building to reap the benefit of this modern technology was the workhouse, being directly in the path of the first line that was run to the village. At first, the capability extended only to the provision of electric light, which spread from the South Mill along Salisbury Road and Salisbury Street, branching west down Church Street, east along High Street and round to the cinema. The demand for electricity was ever increasing, necessitating the provision of additional generating plant. The capacity of the water power being eventually taken up, oil engines had to be installed as well. In 1932 the Company was taken over by the Mid-Southern Utilities. By 1935 all the generators at the mill were running at full capacity. Not another volt could be produced, nor was there room to install additional equipment. It was, therefore, fortuitous that the Wessex Electricity Company appeared on the scene, in the form of a 33 kV alternating current supply line from their station at Wilton, overland to Andover, passing close to South Mill. This line possessed sufficient spare capacity for Amesbury to benefit and the situation was saved. In 1945 the Amesbury Electric Light Company came into the hands of the Wessex Electricity Company and, now stretched to the limit, began to run down, not able any longer to meet the still rising demand for electricity. In 1948 the Wessex Electricity Company became nationalised, eventually becoming the Southern Electricity Board.

All that remains of the once extensive gravel workings.

Salisbury Road   At the top of South Mill Road, at its junction with Salisbury Road, stands the modern police station, erected with the adjacent home for elderly persons on the site of former farm buildings in 1976. It represents the latest stage of keeping the locals in order, although nowadays the local community probably represents the least problem to the Amesbury police. The building contains two items of carved stone-work, removed from the former Edwardian style police station in School Lane that it replaces. A carved crest can be seen on the outer south wall and a reproduction of Stonehenge is situated within the front entrance.

Here also is the later of Amesbury's tollhouses. This one, built in 1836, is positioned at the junction of the turnpike and the earlier road, to take tolls from those travelling on the new turnpike between Amesbury and Old Sarum.

Nearer to Amesbury is Red House, the former farm house and part of the reorganisation that appears to have evolved from the process of enclosure. It is an 18th century building in brick, with a moulded stone string-course and many other points of architectural character. It retains today only a walled garden and paddock as a reminder of the era in which it formed the focal point of a sizeable country farm.

The 18th century Red House, photographed here in 1915.

A 19th century view of Viney's (formerly Vinons) Farm House.

Next to this lies Antrobus House. Another red-brick building, this one was erected in 1924, following the death of Colonel Sir Edmund Antrobus. It fulfilled the function of meeting hall and museum, the latter containing items of local origin and also those collected by the Antrobus family during their various travels. The museum no longer exists, the first floor room now being the meeting place of the Parish Council. The ground floor hall with its stage still caters for public functions.

Across the road is the 17th century Viney's Farm House, possibly the oldest house in the village. Known originally as Vinon's farm house it still bears the name of the family for so long associated with it and with the village. Reduced to the status of farm cottages during the first half of the 20th century, its present use as an art and craft centre helps to restore to it some of its former quality.

The other trackway joining the Salisbury Road at its junction with South Mill Road brought people from Porton, as its name implied. This track drops down over the southern scarp at the eastern edge of the Lynchets.

Earls Court Road and Parsonage Lane   The last route from the south brought people from Newton Toney, Allington and Idmiston to the weekly markets, the fairs and the festivals. These individual routes merged and eventually entered Amesbury as the 18th century Bakers Lane or, to give it its present name, Earls Court Road.

The principal building in this road, apart from the primary school of Christ the King, is the early 19th-century Earls Court Farmhouse, another product of the land enclosure process. A little of the earlier character of the road can still be seen in the two 18th-century cottages—one brick and chalk, the other cob and thatch—about fifty metres to the north and south of the farmhouse. Other cottages were lost when the road was widened earlier this century.

In between this road and the South Mill-Salisbury Road complex lay Bartnett Field, separated from the village in the 18th century by Parsonage Lane. Still known as Parsonage Road, the full significance of the name is now lost but, until the mid-1950's, the road contained at its mid-point Parsonage Barn, a wood and thatched structure of 18th century character, which was demolished to make way for the playing field of Christ the King Catholic School. The barn and the road had been so named for at least 200 years. A Parsonage Close existed in Earls Court Road during the early 18th century.

It is possible that these sites were all that remained of the glebe land or, alternatively, may have evolved from former holdings of the monastic community. This latter possibility may be enhanced by the presence of Black Cross Field, a name associated with a religious site or holding, which joins Bartnett Field at its southern edge. However, by the mid 19th century only Parsonage Road remains of that name; the other references had gone and did not even appear in the tithe award map, suggesting that all ecclesiastical connections, if they had ever existed, had ceased by that time. Today, the northern part of Bartnett Field adjoining Parsonage Road, contains a Council housing estate dating mainly from the 1930's intersected by the linking Highfield, Lynchfield and Lynchets Roads.

North

Keeping to the north-south theme for the moment, primary access to Amesbury from the north after the early 19th century was along the Countess Road of today, following the high ground on the western side of the river. Prior to this, access would have been along what is now the Old Marlborough Road, through Bulford and Ratfyn to the village. Additional access existed as a branch from the Devizes to Salisbury road, to the west of Amesbury. Minor tracks also existed, joining the local villages and hamlets.

Countess Road   Countess Road seems to have assumed its present importance only since the turnpike era. Its age is not certain; it may have been the 18th century Dark Lane, referred to in the manorial court records but it would appear to be of some antiquity. Dropping down from the high ground to the north of the village at the manorial boundary, it descended to the lower ground of the river valley through steep banks forming a narrow passage. Now broadened, hard surfaced and forced to conform to 20th century requirements, a glimpse of its early character can be seen at the tollhouse which was built in approximately 1765. Here, the original road level can be deduced from the drop to the doorstep.

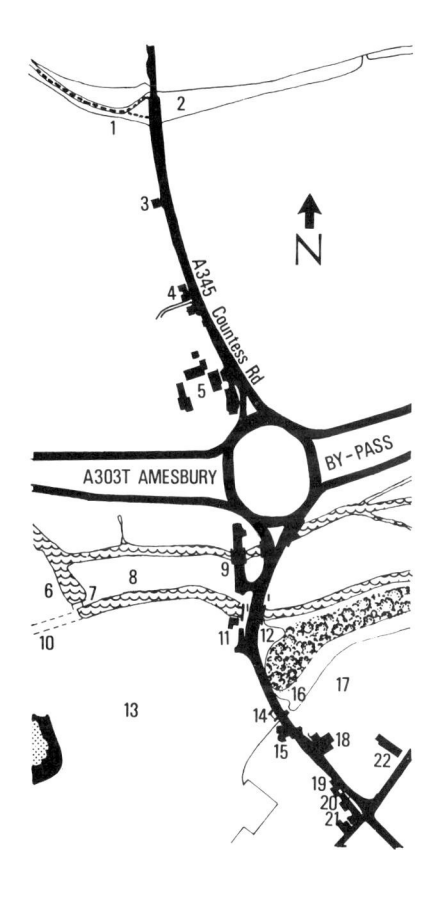

1 Former military railway, now public path to Larkhill, etc.
2 Route of former military railway
3 Toll-house
4 Farm cottages
5 Countess Farm
6 Upper Folds
7 Bowles hatches
8 Lower Folds
9 Northern Graybridge
10 Course of former canal
11 Diana House
12 Gray Bridge Hill
13 Abbey Park
14 Abbey gates
15 Kent House
16 Lord's Walk
17 Town-End Little Field
18 Druids Restaurant
19 Comilla House and stables
20 Post Office
21 Hardware shop
22 Roman Catholic Church

The bank at this point had formerly a similar one on the east side of the road, situated more or less where the present road centre lies.

The first building to be seen on this route into Amesbury during the 18th century would have been the tollhouse with its turnpike gate and adjacent farm cottages. Today, of course, almost the entire length of the road is built up with a 20th century ribbon development not too favoured by present planners.

North of the river, the oldest buildings apart from the tollhouse are the barns and house of Countess Farm. The front portion of the house is late 18th century but this seems to be a later addition to the rear half, the steep roof pitch of which was designed to take thatch, the general character suggesting an early 18th century date, or possibly even a little earlier.

The adjacent 18th-century traditional barns are kept in such excellent condition by a caring owner. The barn to the south of the house has the year of construction 1772 inscribed by its builder J. Osgood, thought to have been a Cholderton man.

The 18th century toll-house in Countess Road, erected by the Amesbury Turnpike Trust.

Countess Farm House and barn.

Estate cottages and bridge in Countess Road. The cottages were demolished when the A303 Amesbury by-pass was constructed. The area is now a layby at the junction with the A345.

At this point however, any original character of the road has been swept away by the modern junction roundabout with the A303. The character is partially restored on the southern side of the roundabout where the former road exists now as a layby at the west side of the new road. The predecessor to the stone bridge here was the "norther gray-bridge" of the 1639 perambulation where, after running north from the village along the roadway, the boundary between the Priory and Earldom Manors turned west to follow the centre of the river, passing the Upper and Lower Folds on the south bank until turning north again at Bocker Mead after two furlongs. Crossing the river and following the present road into Amesbury leads to the ascent of the scarp formed by the river meanderings. Here are two buildings constructed during the 17th century in the Earl of Hertford's period of ownership. The buildings are of similar character, showing good stonework, unusual architectural features in the form of the octagonal towers with their ogee roofs and a considerable extent of knapped flintwork ranging from superior to mediocre. The building at the bottom of the hill is inscribed and dated "Diana her Hous 1600". Kent House, at the top of the hill, is dated 1607. The precise purpose of Diana House is uncertain but various possibilities have been suggested—boating house, hunting lodge, gazebo or even the residence of some official of the estate. It appears originally to have stood just outside the estate wall. Its presence close to the river and to an earlier road bridge that has since been modified may be significant. The dedication of the house to the goddess of hunting may also be a key to its existence.

Ascending the hill into Amesbury we come to the second of these distinctive buildings. This one has been appreciably enlarged over the years as can be seen from the varying standards of flintwork, comparison of the present plan with that in the 18th century map and by the changes in architectural features. This was the gatehouse for the 17th century and former primary entrance to the abbey park, as can be seen from the adjacent gates. The main approach to the park was from the east, along Lord's Walk, formerly Lord Carleton's Walk, from the owner who greatly influenced the layout of the grounds during the early part of the 18th century. One's presence in Lord's Walk today does not readily permit the visualisation of an impressive approach to the abbey, although the remains of the twin rows of trees that flanked the former driveway do still lend a certain grandeur to the scene. Once inside the gates the vista improved, with the regimented lines of lime trees leading to the mansion but today this entrance is of minor importance and sees little use. The gatehouse here, known as Kent House, was also the farm house of the Park Farm.

It is just a short step now to the end of this road, at its junction with the London Road. The orchards that formerly lined the route here are gone. On the west side is the walled garden of Comilla House, the wall being constructed in traditional local character, a chequer of brick, flint and chalk block. Much repaired over the years and covered with grime its true character is becoming a little difficult to discern and its present wavering line suggests that in spite of being protected by law as a structure of historical and architectural interest, it will not be with us for much longer. Opposite this the present Druids restaurant replaces the earlier Smokey Joe's and Millards Cafe of the post-war era and the Colonial Restaurant of the early years of this century. The thatched cottages at the north-east corner of the junction disappeared around 1920, leaving only Comilla House opposite, part of the former New Inn, to indicate some of the former character of this area. Careful study of this house shows many alterations that have taken place over the years to convert the style from country inn to well appointed house. The adjacent garage and outhouse, former doctor's surgery, show some superior chalk block construction.

Diana House and Countess Road as they appeared up to the late 1960's.

The changes brought by the by-pass can be seen in this illustration. The quiet rural setting of Diana House has been eroded by the demands of modern road transport.

A view today of the north entrance to the town central area, with the 17th century abbey park lodge, later Park Farm House and now Kent House, at the right.

East

Prior to the 18th century a traveller approaching Amesbury from the east would come uphill from Cholderton and swing west over Haradon Hill, now Beacon Hill. He would have been presented with a barren view, all traces of the village again being hidden in the river valley. The undulating scrub and grass covered Plain stretched before him with only grazing cattle, the large flocks of sheep with their attendant shepherds clad sometimes in rough white cloaks to greet the eye.

By the 18th century agriculture had become more centralised than that of earlier periods as can be witnessed by the various groups of "Celtic" field systems still defined in the present landscape. A reminder of those times when local inhabitants were grouped into smaller and more widespread communities from which our present system has evolved. This east-west route, having stood the comings and goings of man since earliest times, must have seen many such changes in the agricultural scene as owners, fashions, methods and the levels of civilisation varied, one hopes improving over the years!

In inclement weather, the traveller could branch right in a northerly direction instead of descending into Amesbury and take the higher ground through Bulford and on westwards along the Packway through Shrewton. Alternatively, he could approach the village along the London Way which corresponds to the present A303. Until the by-pass was built in 1970 one would cross the road to Bulford at Folly Bottom before ascending the final rise into the eastern end of the town to join the London Road. Access to the village from the east today can be via three routes, of which the London Road is the major. The other two are Kitchener Road and the Drove.

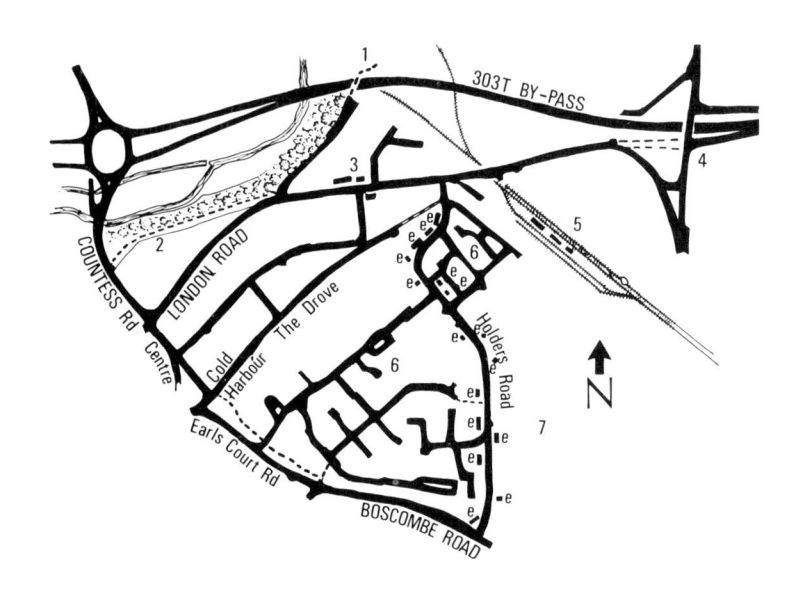

1 Ratfyn
2 Lord's Walk
3 Concrete Bungalows
4 Folly Bottom
5 Railway Station
6 Farm Holdings (Now Local Authority Housing Estate)
7 Farm Holdings
e Experimental Houses

The Railway In 1902 a distraction appeared on the hitherto relatively tranquil scene in the form of the railway, of which practically all trace has disappeared now. The station lay to the south of London Road, at its east end, on the site that the Amesbury Transport Company and other local light industries occupy today. The line passed north-south under the road with the single track to Bulford and beyond curving eastwards on its embankment as it passed Ratfyn Farm. Provision of this amenity became feasible only after the Basingstoke to Salisbury line was authorised in 1854. Suddenly, access to London and beyond was becoming easily available. Horizons receded for trade and travel and thus began the decline of market and fair as they had been established for centuries. First attempts to provide rail transport met with no success. A line planned to run through Amesbury, Shrewton, Westbury and eventually reach Bristol was defeated in Parliament in 1883 by opposition from the Great Western Railway which held a virtual monopoly of traffic from London. A further proposal in 1896 for a north-south route following the Avon valley and serving Salisbury, the Woodfords, Durnford, West Amesbury, Amesbury and onwards to Durrington and eventually Pewsey met with opposition from the War Office as such a route would bisect its newly acquired training area on Salisbury Plain.

These two views reflect the normal rural tranquillity of Amesbury's railway station between the wars.

65

The line which was the outcome of all this wrangling was largely instigated by the military authorities which probably accounted for its bias towards a service from London rather than a local catchment area. Public traffic commenced in 1902, by the London and South Western Railway. Two years later the junction with the Salisbury-Basingstoke line was improved to allow easy access to Salisbury. This permitted the setting-up of a useful local service at a time when road transport was still in its infancy.

The strategic importance of the railway did not, of course, escape the notice of the Army. At the outbreak of the first world war a further line was constructed from Amesbury to serve Larkhill, Stonehenge airfield, Rollestone balloon school and the other military establishments at that time on the Plain which had begun to feel the effects of concentrated troop training. This military line commenced at Ratfyn, crossed the river valley to Countess Road by viaduct and proceeded north-west towards Larkhill, etc. It was taken up in 1937, rail activity reverting to primarily passenger and freight services between Salisbury, Amesbury and Bulford plus the other intervening villages. Passenger traffic continued until 1952 and freight until 1963 when the line was closed as part of the economy measures.

The railway station grew very quickly from its original modest country status, being rapidly enlarged to cope with the wartime requirement, its four platforms at times being packed with military personnel. It declined in its later years, assuming again its rural characteristics, with only the turntable, unused marshalling tracks and extensive signalling to tell of the former activities.

The railway finally closed down in 1965 when the permanent way, despite the title, was taken up. The station, bridges and buildings are gone but the Ratfyn siding remains outlined, although truncated by the by-pass, a reminder of its presence shown by the east wall of the former Home Farm Model Dairies, the construction of which had to depart from the orthogonal norm. The railway staff cottages built solidly of red brick in typical style still stand at the entrance to the transport yard, outshone by the relative magnificence of the former station-master's house on the corner of London Road and Holders Road. The routes of the two railways can still be traced fairly easily, some lengths now being public rights of way.

Holders Road   Although it does not give access to the village, this is probably a convenient moment to consider Holders Road. It originally linked the east end of London Road with the road leading up from Amesbury to Boscombe Down. Now it gives access also to the various Council estates along its route.

Holders Road contains houses that are probably unique to Amesbury. Erected just after the first world war by the Ministry of Agriculture and Fisheries in conjunction with the Department of Science and Industrial Research the houses were intended as an experimental examination of various almost forgotten rural building methods and tests of new materials, methods and apparatus.

The project resulted from the requirements of the Land Settlement Act and included with each house sufficient land for a small-holding, from which the road name is derived. The holdings were made available to those returning from the war.

There were approximately 14 single houses and 18 pairs of cottages, utilising revived old methods, new methods and normal methods of the time. These included pisé de terre, chalk cob, weatherboard with timber frame, brick and

Then and now—how the experimental houses and their environment in Holders Road have matured since 1920.

concrete. Converted army sectional huts were also included in the scheme, to ensure that every avenue was explored!

Fifty years later they are all, apart from one, standing as firm as ever. That which is lost was vandalised after being left vacant. There is no building method yet devised that is immune to that particular process!

Kitchener Road This road is of relatively recent origin, having evolved during the 20th century from a trackway leading to a copse and pig farm, to a metalled road feeding a high density estate which was previously a site for mobile and other temporary forms of accommodation up to the 1950's.

The Drove and Coldharbour   The Drove appears to have appreciably earlier origins. Although now associated with just another building estate with the right of common way reduced to a footpath's width, it was originally at least 150 feet wide in places, enough for the vast flocks of sheep and cattle to be brought from the downs into the village market and beyond into new pastures. The Drove is first identifiable at the point where it leaves Holders Road, just off the London Road. Its original width can be seen in the depth of the gardens plus the footpath and road of the same name. Entering Coldharbour from the east, the wide road was gradually encroached upon by the mud-walled cottages of farm tenants erected on waste ground in the roadway during the 18th and 19th centuries, the infant school premises, council dwellings and bungalows in the early 20th century to become the metalled Coldharbour road of today. Both the Drove and Kitchener Road contained extensive allotment areas, evident here since the 19th century and only fairly recently declining in popularity.

The London Road   The London Road, in common with the Countess and Salisbury Roads, exhibits the "ribbon" development characteristics by which a growing community during the early 20th century was able to house its increasing populace, bringing with it the diversity of architectural styles established before the more formalised planning regulations evolved.

The earlier lack of planning control has left the east end of London Road something of a disaster area, containing decaying tin huts, a redundant petrol filling station and other utilitarian commercial establishments that blend to give the area a distinct second-rate impression. In addition, the large NAAFI complex looms darkly at the Folly Bottom approach, an unfortunate example of planning with complete disregard to the surrounding environment. Thankfully the situation does recover itself somewhat as one nears the village. The first notable inclusion

Coldharbour in 1934. The cob-walled cottages are built along the centre of the old drove-way.

Coldharbour today—all the cottages are gone, only the bungalow remaining from the previous photograph.

on the scene is the single storied flat-roofed bungalows; built in eastern style during the 1920s by the local entrepreneur "Bungy" Woods of whom we have spoken earlier, they are in fact interesting examples of an early rural application of reinforced concrete. Mr. Woods, always a resourceful man, collected together whatever metalwork he thought would be useful as a reinforcing agent, and it has been observed that this included the various parts of early aircraft.

About half-way along the road one meets the easterly entrance to Lord's Walk, still marked by the large tumulus residing in the adjacent garden. Here also is the entrance to Ratfyn Road, the earlier main entrance to the village from the north, now a private road but with a public right of way that still permits access to the neighbouring village of Bulford along much the same route as before. Further along towards the village is the Roman Catholic Church, founded in 1934. We stop, a little further on, at the crossroads, with YMCA establishment and garages replacing the earlier cottages and dwellings removed during the turnpiking era.

Bungy Woods' concrete bungalows, more officially described as "interesting Neo-Renaissance one-storey residences".

West

Access to Amesbury from the west has seen much modification over the years. Today one approaches on the A303 by-pass, passing through beech clumps attractively positioned to represent the British and French ships at the Battle of the Nile in 1798; to the right is the Iron Age hillfort known erroneously as Vespasian's Camp.

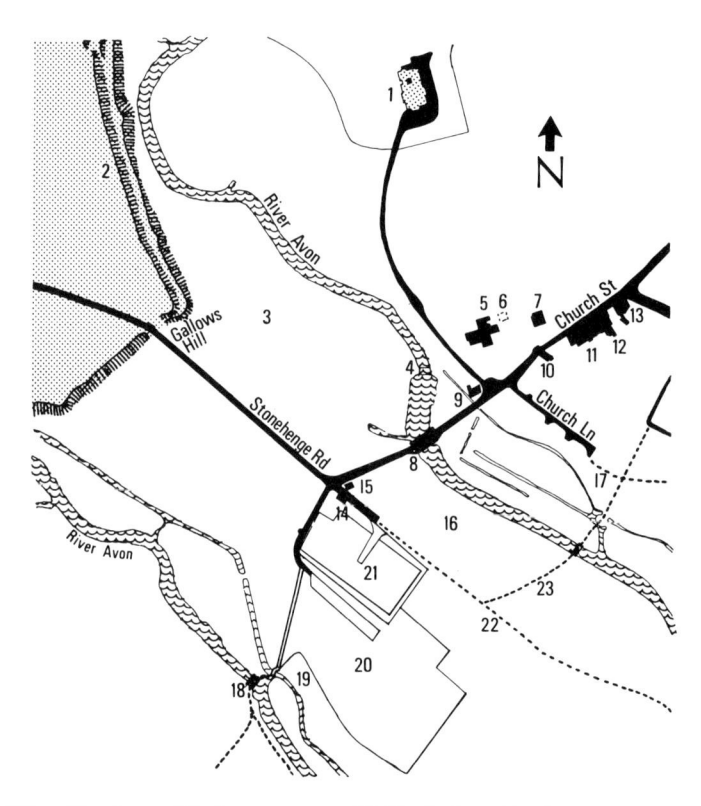

1 The Abbey Mansion and Park
2 Vespasian's Camp boundary
3 Water meadows
4 Queens Falls weir
5 Parish Church of St Mary and St Melor
6 Site of former vicarage
7 Present vicarage
8 Queensberry Bridge, or Great Bridge
9 Tumbling Bay
10 The Phoenix
11 Antrobus Arms Hotel (also former vicarage and school)
12 King's Arms Hotel
13 Lloyds Bank and site of former Market House
14 Little Thatch cottage
15 Site of toll-house
16 Water meadows
17 Almanaze path
18 Ham hatches
19 Bonney Mead
20 Recreation Ground
21 Cemetery
22 Wittenham path
23 Approximate route of Broad Bridge road

Stonehenge Road   Prior to the construction of the by-pass in 1970 to enter the village from the west one would leave the present route of the A303 close to the first of the beech clumps and bear right, down the hill, into the village, past the rather fine milestone which, bearing the date 1764 reminds one of the turnpike era. This portion of road now allows only one-way through traffic, permitting one to leave the village and join the westbound A303; two-way traffic is resumed from the junction with the West Amesbury road. This area has gained the name of Gallows Hill, the reason in this particular case not being clear as no references have been found to show the execution of local justice here, hanging being beyond the normal terms of reference of the manorial court. It has been speculated that the name is derived from the memory of some local tragedy. The road into Amesbury cuts through the west portion of Vespasian's Camp with dwellings ranging from modest to relatively grandiose lining the west bank.

Another, more localised, approach to Amesbury from the westerly direction is represented by the various rights of way from West Amesbury, Normanton and Durnford all of which cross the Avon at Ham Hatches, skirting the recreation ground along its northern edge and meeting the former turnpike road at Cemetery Corner. The importance of these paths has long since declined. Once they would have permitted the labourers access to their strips of land, allowed the shepherd to drive sheep to the downs and seen much traffic to Dawbony's Mill which appears to have stood in the vicinity of Ham Hatches.

West Amesbury House: principally 16th to 17th century construction in chequer stone and flint; contains traces of an older building thought to have been associated with Amesbury's monastic house.

The peaceful hamlet of West Amesbury has not changed much since this scene at the turn of the century.

Up to the early part of the 17th century this entrance to the village appears to have continued in a southerly direction from Cemetery Corner. By 1675 a wooden bridge was constructed approximately on the site of the present stone bridge which superseded it in 1775, allowing the road to take its present line. The route of the earlier road can be seen in the line of the present Wittenham footpath which has evolved from an 18th century access road. Following the footpath south for approximately 150 yards one would then turn eastwards, crossing the river at Broad Bridge, entering the village via Frog Lane. By the early 18th century the bridge was gone, remembered only by the field name which led to the river. While Broad Bridge existed it must have provided a principal westerly access to the village, possibly for cattle and sheep, its continuation to Frog Lane giving direct access to the market. This busy area could be avoided for through traffic by branching right into the later Tanners Lane, the present southerly half of Flower Lane. The approach road to Broad Bridge became a cul-de-sac, giving access to the fields and water meadows. Either the shallowness of the river at that point permitted it to be forded, or a more circuitous route may have been adopted, using the Wood-Way from Durnford, approaching Amesbury along the west bank of the river from Ham Hatches around to South Mill. Alternatively, a route may have existed to the north of Vespasian's Camp, joining Countess Road at some point as indicated by pre by-pass paths, but this is somewhat speculative.

The toll-house and adjacent cottage, formerly Pink House school, at the south end of Stonehenge Road. The principal route turns left, passing the front of the toll-house at the left of the picture. The former road continued between the two buildings and is now known as the Wittenham path.

CHAPTER NINE: AMESBURY CHURCH

Introduction

The church that we see today is a large building for a community of such relatively modest size. It is a building that has slowly evolved into its present form. To do justice to its antiquity and character a detailed description has been attempted. A close inspection of the building will reveal the many alterations that have taken place which reflect the changing demands made upon it over the centuries. The church consists principally of a 12th century nave, with transepts, chapel, tower and chancel of late 12th to early 13th century date. In addition to its role as a place of Christian worship it has been meeting place, school, refuge and store and still stands today as an example of the highest aspirations of this little community. Its precise link with the monastic house, remains of which were found at the west end of the nave and several hundred yards to the north, is still an unanswered question but the proximity in the 18th century of a water mill and several other large buildings of agricultural nature lends substance to the theory that it may have evolved from the early monastic church, later becoming that of the parish as well.

One's first impression is of a church built principally from local stone on the Latin cross plan with a central crossing tower which dominates not so much by its height but by its massive proportion. Add to it the octagonal spire which may have adorned the church until the dissolution, and other missing portions to the church and one has a building not unimpressive in size and complexity. The traditional steep pitch of the original roof, so well designed for the prevailing weather conditions, can be seen by the slope of the roof line mouldings above the present tiles. As lead came more into use, from the 13th century onwards, the steep pitch was reduced to that seen in the nave roof; although the former eaves have been retained, the more normal parapet was not incorporated for some reason. Later work restored the pitch of the transept and chancel roofs. At the south-west side of the church let into the wall one can see the shed, or outhouse, constructed from many of the parts that Butterfield found surplus, rather like the pieces left over from a clock repaired by an inexperienced hand! Left with a pile of stones he chose a hopefully redeeming action! The wall itself is worth just a mention. Half way along, near to the war memorial, a discontinuity formed by stone blocks can be seen. This feature relates quite accurately in position to the corner of one of the large buildings on the 1726 map of the village. Hence it is possible that the portion of this towards the church formed the lower part of an earlier east wall of quite a sizeable building—possibly a tithe barn.

The Exterior

To look at the church more closely walk around the outside, starting at the present main entrance, the south transept door.

The South Transept   The present south face of this transept was designed by the eminent Victorian architect William Butterfield who did so much either to enhance the building, or to degrade it if the Victorian Gothic style does not appeal.

Up to 1853, when the alterations were made, this south face was in the Renaissance style containing a door positioned much as the present one, a single lancet window centrally above, with a circular opening over that, the whole being surmounted by the sundial that is retained. It is thought that this former facade originated in 1723.

The east wall of the south transept shows the former existence of another chapel, illustrated by the roof-line and the blocked arch now pierced by a 15th century window. The misalignment between the roof moulding and the arch is curious, suggesting two different periods of use, the arch tending to align itself with the grooving in the angle buttress of the tower and hence perhaps being the later of the two features, which have never received an adequate explanation. The 15th century window inserted in the blocked arch appears again as the product of either hasty workmanship or outwards pressure from the weight of the tower, the jamb and mullions having strayed visibly from the vertical. A lancet window serves to break the monotony of the remainder of this wall and is the survivor of two, the other being blocked in the opposite wall.

The seal of Isabel de Geneville, elected Prioress at Amesbury in 1309. It depicts the prioress kneeling, with the king, seated, above. The building at the top is a possible representation of Amesbury's monastic church at that time.
Reproduced by courtesy of the Society of Antiquaries of London.

The church prior to its restoration by Butterfield. This 18th century view shows the former vicarage, now demolished, which was thought to be part of the monastic buildings. The fence was removed by the Turnpike Trust in 1826 when the road was widened.

Continuing around the church in a westerly direction, one can see on the west wall of the south transept much evidence of the periodic repair and patching that has taken place over the years. The blocked 13th century lancet window has given way to a "Classical" version of the 18th century which has itself been blocked with flint. The possibility that the Romanesque building incorporated transepts that were re-worked into the later 13th century structure is suggested by the 12th century flat buttress now partially concealed at the corner made by the transept and south aisle.

The South Aisle The south side along the length of the nave is in the 15th century Perpendicular style, replacing its 12th century forerunner, the irregularities in the window masonry exhibiting somewhat hasty execution of the task of insertion. The large Tudor style door at the west end was, until the 19th century, under the cover of a large stone porch of uncertain age.

The west end of the church is reached through the gate in the wall.

The Nave At the west end of the church one can see again the evidence of much change. The west wall of the nave is by Butterfield, his windows replacing an earlier three-light Perpendicular style window. On the upper portion of the nave west wall before it joins the south aisle one can see the several dripstone lines left without a function as a result of alteration. Also visible at the top of the wall, just under the roof line, are weather-worn corbels. If this church is the building described as the monastery church at the dissolution, then the nave would have been approximately twice its present length. Certainly the present vertical dimensions give the existing structure a somewhat truncated look, not pleasing to the eye. The position of the portion of richly shafted early 13th century doorway protruding from the west end of the nave may be misleading as it is thought to be reset. As presently orientated its use as an entrance would take one away from the nave. Excavations in 1920 established what was thought to be Saxon door footings aligned with, but about a foot away from, the nave north wall. Recent work has shown them to be of a later period, and positioned at an angle of approximately $5°$ to the nave, suggesting a separate building to the present structure.

Continuing on round the end of the nave to its north wall, further evidence of the Norman period can be seen in the weather-worn corbel table under the eaves and also in the blocked window arches. The two existing windows are in the later, Perpendicular, style. The unfortunate but main feature of this wall is the Victorian "crazy-paving" effect which, as elsewhere on the building, Mr Butterfield seems to have achieved with lasting brilliance.

The horizontal moulded course running along the wall at mid-height has been considered to provide evidence of former cloisters. It seems more likely that a 12th century north aisle or passage of the "lean-to" style is suggested if the slope of the string course on the north transept wall is considered. Cloisters, if any, might have led off from such an aisle if positioned in the usual monastic configuration. The positioning of the later windows high up in the wall would suggest the continuing presence of a north aisle until the 15th century.

The south-east aspect of the church as it appears today. Some of the 19th century alterations made to the chancel and south transept can be seen, by comparing with the previous illustration.

In this view from the north-west the former roof-lines are clearly visible on the tower walls, as are the blocked Norman windows and the north aisle string course in the nave north wall.

The North Transept The north and west walls of the north transept are late 12th to early 13th century in general character and again possess the typical graceful lancet windows of that period. The blocked door in the west wall gives evidence of former passage between the supposed north aisle and the interior of the building. Evidence of former structures, long since disappeared and of unknown purpose, is given by the still visible quoin stones set into the west wall at the transept north-west corner, and by the roll-moulding along the north end, running through the window bases. The east wall of the transept provides a slightly more exciting prospect, apart from the classical lines of the lean-to tool shed. The predominant feature in this wall is the Jesus Chapel, of later date than the main structure as suggested by the partially concealed roll moulding that runs around the north end of the transept. The lower windows of the chapel are Early English lancets but the upper window in the gable is a more ornate affair of plate tracery, with two trefoil-headed lights divided by a small pillar with foliated capital and with a quatrefoil opening in the head. It has been dated as late 13th century and is thought to be reset.

Close to the chancel wall is Mr Butterfield's brick and sandstone gothic style turret staircase, surmounted by its fine wrought-iron cross enriched with blacksmith's scrollwork. It replaces the earlier interior staircase and leads to the ringing floor of the bell-tower. An external access to the present turret has apparently been bricked up. Partially obscured by the turret is the blocked archway with roof moulding that would have led from the north transept to a side chapel or vestry for the chancel. This aisle has, of course, long since disappeared but ample evidence remains; for instance the blocked lower portions of the 13th century lancet windows and the blocked 13th century door with its nearby aumbry or cupboard, now just a niche in the wall.

The Chancel   The presence of the Decorated window, inserted during the first half of the 14th century, suggests that the chancel side chapel, or vestry, had possibly gone by that time. The fact that this window is not aligned with that of similar period in the south wall may also suggest that the easterly part of the aisle remained at this time. The window is of interesting style, being a fine example of reticulated tracery. It is possible that it was executed by a west country mason, as he introduced into the corbels at the foot of the interior arch the ball-flower ornament so popular in Gloucestershire and Somerset during this period. Little work of the 14th century exists in the church. An angle or 'French' buttress exists at the north-east corner of the chancel, a variation not introduced to England until the 14th century. It was built probably at the time that the aisle was removed. The remaining buttresses on this side date from the Victorian period and became necessary only then to lend support to the bulging chancel walls. The east end of the chancel received attention from Mr Butterfield during his restoration work of 1853. Prior to this time the east wall contained a large five-light Perpendicular window attributed to the early 15th century period. For reasons unknown but presumably its poor condition, it was replaced by the window present today. It must be said in Butterfield's favour that he appears to have retained the ashlar face and to have effected this part of his work without scarring the overall character too deeply. Continuing on round the building, the same architectural theme is continued in the south face of the chancel, the ashlar work in the upper part this time contrasting with the lower rubble walling that would originally have been plastered over, not coming into favour until the 19th century.

The line of the graceful 13th century lancet windows in the south wall is broken by the later insertion of the Decorated window, of earlier style than that in the north wall. This one is a rather nice example of cusped intersected tracery, with a large pointed quatrefoil spreading out at the top. A priests door was removed from the centre of this wall in the 19th century and the jamb incorporated either in the coal-shed or in the wall around the present vicarage, the two being sufficiently similar in general shape to make identification difficult from the rather vague drawings that exist.

The Interior

The South Transept   Entering the church by the south transept door, now the principal entrance, there is, to one's left, the 15th century clock mechanism, in use until the early part of this century.

The barrel vault or wagon roof is of the Tudor period, as are those of the north transept and south aisle.

The South Aisle   Passing along the transept, turning left into the south aisle, one can see the richly decorated roof, executed to great effect. Here also is the font, the upper portion of which is 13th century with the typical shallow blank arch decoration, made from Purbeck marble and supported on a later base. This font was broken up by Butterfield and used as rubble beneath the chancel floor, from whence it was recovered during later work at the beginning of this century

The Jesus Chapel, the last remaining side chapel, is situated in the north transept.

The Norman font, reconstructed from fragments retrieved from under the chancel floor.

and used to replace the Victorian version which is thought to have been acquired by one of the neighbouring village churches. In the south wall of the aisle, close to the font, is a piscina, a relic from a former chapel or side altar. Close examination will reveal a particularly poor standard of workmanship in the heads forming the hoodmould stops, as if executed by an extremely inexperienced mason. Another piscina exists in the south wall close to the west door. Nearby is the only locally remaining item retrieved from the excavations of 1860, which brought to light the controversial remains of the monastic house. Described variously as font or lavatorium, its date and precise purpose remain in doubt still.

The Nave Standing at the west end of the nave gives one an idea of the spacious character of the building, particularly if the presence of a former north aisle and a longer nave with its north and south walls pierced with archways is visualised. Further evidence of a north aisle, possibly pre-dating the present nave, is suggested by the pillar base found deep in the north wall at the east end of the nave during the 1920 repairs. The alignment of the pillar is of interest as it does not conform to that of the present nave, but more with that of the chancel which can be seen to be well out of alignment with the nave when viewed from the west end. The south wall of the nave is pierced by a two-bay arcade, leading to the 15th century south aisle. The present arcade probably replaces an earlier

The interior of the church as intended by Butterfield. A spacious arch leading into the chancel with its typically Victorian tiles behind the altar.

The 'St Melor' mural can be seen to the right of the banner at the central pillar, in this present-day view. Also visible is the 15th century chancel screen rescued from destruction.

version which formed part of the Norman nave and which was balanced by a similar structure along the north side, the character of the pillars being perhaps demonstrated by the base set into the north wall. In the upper part of the south wall can be seen the blocked Norman windows which once, before the present aisle was built, would have helped to illuminate an otherwise gloomy nave. Construction of the aisle, with the insertion of these two arches produced stress problems that had not been envisaged by the relatively rudimentary approach to the task. The south-west pier supporting the tower could no longer take the strain and showed its protest by leaning ominously. Support had to be provided rather hastily, which resulted in the somewhat ungainly rectangular addition to this pier. The departure of the tower pier from the vertical can be best seen by viewing it from the west end of the nave, looking towards the chancel and aligning it with the south-east pier or other verticals. The supporting structure has been used to some benefit, as can be seen by the remains of the wall painting on the north face. Thought to represent Saint Melor and of unknown date, it has been reduced by the ravages of time and the application of much whitewash from a full-length figure visible at the turn of the century to the present barely discernible head and shoulders. Such little interest is shown in conserving or protecting what remains of the image that before long it will probably disappear completely under a fresh coat of zealously applied paint. Other decorative points of interest in the nave are the photographs of the 'Amesbury Psalter' on the south wall and the hatchment depicting the coat of arms of the Antrobus family, presumably hung in the church after the bereavement of some member of the family.

The woodwork of the nave roof whilst elaborate has a somewhat makeshift appearance. This has been thought to indicate that it was re-erected after the dissolution from various pieces. This possibility is illustrated by the spacing of the wall corbels, which are positioned awkwardly in relation to the blocked windows on the north side. Additionally, poppy heads are broken from some of the cusps, poor carving is mixed with good and the filling of several of the spandrels is clumsy, differing from the original design.

Before the 19th century restoration the nave contained three galleries, the inferred dimensions of which must have appreciably restricted the space available to the devout community! The largest gallery was situated at the west end of the nave, more or less above the present vestry. It is recorded as projecting far into the church and of having a front painted in black and white stripes. The space beneath was boarded up and used to hoard lumber. In later years, around the mid-19th century, the ground floor area was used as a school. The gallery here, if it followed the normal convention, was probably used by the local musicians, before the advent of the organ. Certainly if the lord of the manor and his guests were in the habit of attending the services a sizeable and relatively proficient orchestra would presumably be expected. Complementing, or competing with, the band of musicians would be the choir which was housed in a sky-blue painted gallery built in 1737 of panelled deal and situated in the easterly of the two archways between the nave and south aisle. It was considered by some to be a clumsy and disfiguring projection. Immediately to the west of this, presumably in the other archway, was an older, private gallery. This was finished in a peach blossom colour lighted by white stripes. The pulpit, complete with massive sounding-board, stood at that time in the nave against the north-west pier of the tower arch. The pulpit was accompanied by the prayer desk and clerk's seat.

The North Transept   The north transept is entered under the organ loft. The two manual electro-pneumatic organ was built in 1888 by Alfred Monk. It is, at the time of writing, in a sad state of repair, having been unable to give full voice for some time. Passing into the north transept one can see on the east wall, half hidden by the organ loft and screen, the blocked arch of the demolished chapel or vestry. The character of the arch is early 13th century, incorporating the typical moulded capitals on their stiff-leaf stops. Similar characteristics are to be seen at the entrance to the one chapel that still remains. The rib-vaulting rising from the slender shafts have foliated caps on the eastern side; there is also a double piscina, again with the stiff-leaf foliation at the hoodmould stops. Traces of red decorative line-work can still just be seen on the stonework in and around the piscina. The cross on the altar is made from oak beams recovered from the foundations during the 19th century work. Traces of a former entrance screen can be observed in the fixing points still visible in the pillars. The north transept was used in the 19th century for the storage of ladders and the fire appliance invented by the Reverend Thomas Holland, in addition to its more usual purpose. Emerging from the north transept, the wooden pulpit with stone base, to one's left, is of Butterfield's Victorian design.

The Chancel   The chancel is entered through a 15th century five-light wooden screen. Much defaced and repaired, the screen has lost the rood-loft that it appears to have once supported. The screen was removed at the time of the 19th century restoration work, but rescued from the scrap heap by Job Edwards, one of Amesbury's former historians, who kept it safe for many years until it could be replaced in 1907. To Butterfield the chancel was the richest part and the focal point of a church. Screens were removed to make it visible, he made its roof the highest in the church and usually he removed all side altars so that a chancel contained the only one. He appears to have relaxed this rule for Amesbury.

The fragments of coloured glass-work in the large windows of the north wall are mostly random pieces. An early 14th century head and shoulders has been preserved intact, and depicts the crowned head of a woman thought to be St. Mary, although Queen Guinevere has been considered a possibility. The remaining fragments of stained glass are of various dates and include 13th century hatched grisaille pieces and Lombardic lettering, plus a small 16th century quarry below the top trefoil.

To the north of the altar is the interior portion of the blocked doorway, with its hoodmould and characteristic stiff-leaf stops; here also is a small but unusually ornate arch, or niche, of the early to mid-14th century period. Canopied and crocketed, with openwork cusping and buttress shafts, it retains the Decorated feeling but exhibits inferior workmanship. It has been postulated that the clumsy design and poor carving resulted from the dearth of competent and progressive masons following the Black Death. If true, this might also account for the crude carving of the piscina near the font.

Behind the altar, Mr Butterfield's tiling and marble panelling remain painted over and hidden from view by the wall-hangings. Perhaps one day, when the work of his period becomes more acceptable to Amesbury, it will again be exposed for all to see. To the south of the altar, the credence table is supported by the external hoodmould stops from the Perpendicular east window removed in the 19th century. They take the form of angels bearing carved escutcheons on which are worked in red and black clay the initials D K D interlaced with a cord.

A most important body of men — the team of bell-ringers!

The principal initial K has been linked with the name Kent as there was, among the buildings of the monastery, an apartment known as Kent's Chamber. According to the Reverend Ruddle, the canopied manor pew was situated at the south side of the chancel, just within the screen. The chancel walls at this point today bear the memorial tablets to members of the Antrobus family, the last and current manorial holders. A continuation of the now faint decorative red lining can be seen on the upper stonework surface of the south wall. The stained glass in the south-east lancet windows is of relatively recent date. The roof was restored by Butterfield to the original 13th century pitch.

The Tower   The crossing tower is supported by four triple-chamfered arches. The south-west pier differs from the others, being embellished with Perpendicular-style panelling. A scratched symbol, suggesting a merchant's mark, is repeated on some of the stones. Near to the south-east pier are some carved stone fragments in a glass case. The principal feature of these is the portion of Saxon wheel-cross.

The Saxon Cross   The cross was recovered from under the chancel floor during restoration work in 1907. It may represent Amesbury's earliest link with Christianity. It exhibits a high standard of workmanship and possesses several interesting characteristics but being still the subject of current research its full import is not yet known. The fact that it was found under the chancel floor suggests that it was one of the items discarded by Butterfield along with the font although, of course, it may well have found its way there from earlier workings or burials, or even from a building pre-dating the present church. It does not appear as an external

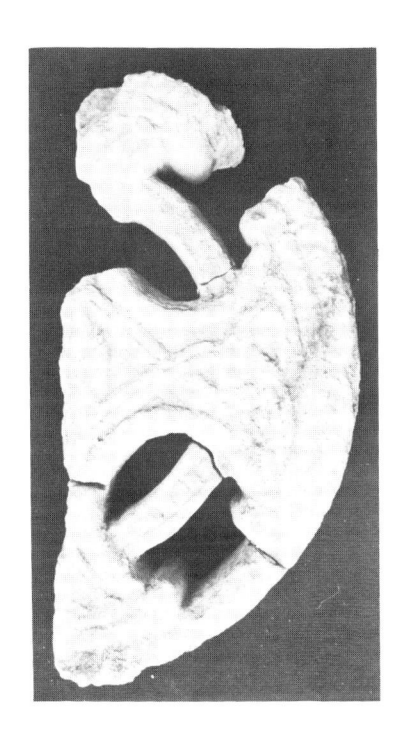

This reconstruction shows the principal design detail.

The Saxon cross fragments.

85

feature on the church in pre-restoration illustrations, which leads one to think that it has an association with some earlier structure. The weathered condition of the cross shows that it was an external feature. The incorporation of the wheel-head suggests an influence from the Irish Sea region via the north-west of England. A direct link with Ireland is suggested by the rolls at the ends of the cross arms where they join the outer ring. It has been dated by various authorities as being 9th to early 11th century, the latter being cautiously considered the more likely. Only one other known cross has a similar cable pattern of linked triquetras and that is at Cardinham in Cornwall.

Bosses and Corbels   Before leaving the church the corbels and ceiling bosses merit examination, if the spine will permit!

The nave roof is supported at its corners by four corbels that take the shape of human figures who are obviously, from their facial expressions, aware of the serious nature of their task in keeping the woodwork in its rightful place. Here also is Abraham, releasing the ram from the bush; a cardinal and a bishop thought to represent Cardinal Carpaccio and Bishop Beauchamp, 14th century figures. Nearby a regal figure, possibly either King Arthur or Ambrosius Aurelianus appears close to the west end. Of the bosses in the woodwork, there is some floral decoration and a horned devil emitting tongues of flame. The corbels and bosses in the south aisle can be more plainly seen; humorously grotesque heads, human figures and flowers. In the south transept are knights—possibly one-time benefactors or local persons; a monster head devouring a man grimly represents Judas Iscariot in the jaws of Satan; another, equally menacing head, grips a large bone between its prominent teeth. The faithful few were left in no doubt of the fate that would befall them if they transgressed! In the north transept religious practices have been conducted on a much more formal basis, under the watchful and uniform gaze of six disapproving angels clutching escutcheons.

Grotesquely carved roof bosses, such as those shown here, served to remind wayward members of the congregation of the perils that awaited if their attentions should wander. Other carvings depicted local worthies, legendary figures and biblical scenes.

Conclusion

As we have seen, the building has been subjected to much modification over the years, the periods of which, as dictated by the architectural styles imposed, tend to coincide with the known periods of rebuilding or alteration in the monastic house. Apart from the nave, the dimensions given for the roofs that were stripped of lead at the time of the dissolution agree fairly well with the relevant dimensions in the present church. The reason for the removal of the structures on the north side of the church is not known but it appears to have occurred prior to the 15th century, in which period a change of use, or emphasis, seems to have occurred, with the main access to the church being transferred to the south side. This is perhaps connected with the removal of the male brethren and the severing of links with France. A move is possibly reflected by the absence of any graves 'behind' the present church and the earliest graves around the front appearing, as far as can be ascertained, not to pre-date this period.

So, until further evidence comes to light, the precise relationship of the present church to the abbey must remain a mystery, and the question prompted by the discovery of the remains 300 yards to the north that has troubled scholars over the last hundred years must still remain unanswered. One can only say that the size and characteristics of the building, including the now missing portions, do suggest a distinct monastic connection, it being altogether too large for just a simple village church.

CHAPTER TEN: THE CENTRAL AREA

When we examined the approaches to Amesbury, we ended up at the west side of the village. We can start our look at the central area from that point, and begin at the bottom, or west end, of Church Street. Before launching into that account, however, we can use the location with the river, recreation ground and nearby downland, to consider briefly the sporting and leisure activities of the village inhabitants.

Recreation

As we saw in chapter four, the ordinary man led a very hard life. Such social events that occurred during his year must have been very welcome and anticipated with a degree of excitement that is largely lost today. The most important event of the year was the annual fair, held around Michaelmas, at which labourers were engaged or discharged from their employment and livestock was bought and sold. Farmers, labourers, tenants and all would have come to these events from all the surrounding villages to buy, sell or just to gossip and meet friends. No doubt Amesbury would have been packed at such occasions. Earlier, in the medieval period, these events would have included activities of a different nature, with archery practice and other militaristic pastimes. This is reflected in the field named "les Butts". Its precise location is not known but appears to have been around the north side of the manor park where, since the 17th century, the annual fair on Countess Court Fields was held. The site of this event spread to Stonehenge and the Cursus to its north. This was one of four similar events held through the year, the earliest recorded fair being held in 1317 to mark the feast of St. Melor. In addition there were weekly markets held in or adjacent to the village.

By the beginning of the 20th century the fairs and markets had diminished both in number and importance. As social events they had to some extent been replaced by the various sporting pastimes practised. Sporting and leisure activities pursued locally are not really recorded until the 18th century but there is little doubt that what amused the inhabitants here was no different from the general scene elsewhere.

Prior to the Victorian period, available leisure time would have been mostly confined to a Sunday and, from the late 18th century onwards, could well have

Recreational activities were often spontaneous affairs dictated by circumstances, as seen here in 1909 on the frozen river at Lords Walk.

Not quite sport, but the 1910 elections allowed a certain freedom of expression! An interesting point here is the continuation from medieval times of the hobby-horse theme, now largely lost.

Stonehenge was a natural venue for many gatherings well into the 20th century.

been spent near Stonehenge watching or playing in the cricket, football and golf matches that were held there until the early part of the 20th century. The downs from Stonehenge to Beacon Hill were also the scene of coursing meetings, the nationally popular sport prior to fox-hunting. Amesbury boasted the second club to be founded in Wiltshire and such was its fame that the meetings attracted participants from as far as Altcar in Lancashire. So highly prized were the dogs that those superior in the chase were even immortalised in verse. Fishing has also been long established but the present sport stops short of the 18th century fashion for young loach swallowed live with a glass of sack! The river was regarded as a useful source of food until well into the 20th century when it was even then periodically dragged with nets to catch the fish and eels.

By the mid 20th century fox-hunting had waned, coursing was extinct and recreational pursuits had evolved conforming more to the requirements of the working-man. A recreation ground was provided for the public by the Parish Council in the 1920s and now more use was being made of it for the more organised games of football, cricket, bowls and tennis. It was also the home of the annual carnival, except when this was held in the Abbey grounds, and, with the accompanying flower and produce show which allowed a man to express his expertise in coaxing a crop from the soil, acted to some extent as a replacement to the centuries-old fairs. Now even this outlet of self-expression is gone. The recreation ground still lives on and, although some of its usefulness has been replaced by the provision of newer sports facilities at the Holders Road sports centre, it still remains the only location that can cater for the cricket and football matches played regularly and is still a venue for families with young children. It is a pity that some of its former scenic qualities are lacking, through the ravages of Dutch Elm disease and the demands of modern usage.

Church Street

Starting at the westerly end, we have today the thatched cottage originally built on Boney Mead and known in the 19th century as "Pink House". The former preparatory school for Rose's Grammar School it was run by a Miss Mary Sandell in 1821 and by her successors later. Until about 1920 it was accompanied by the westerly of Amesbury's tollhouses, which was situated on the other side of the Wittenham path. Near here also were the wooden hutted offices of Bungy Woods' gravel pits, with the narrow gauge railway leading away to the south alongside the path to the gravel pits next to the present effluent disposal plant.

Proceeding towards the town centre the stone bridge is crossed which, as we have seen earlier, when built in 1775 following the institution of the turnpikes, greatly facilitated access to Amesbury from the west. A little further along the street, by the small stone bridge carrying a former mill leet later to be used to control the water meadows as well, is the most recent of the abbey park gatehouses. Used as such since the southern entrance to the park was constructed in the mid 18th century, the gate piers with their Doric columns and adjacent wall are 17th century and were moved to the present site from nearer the former abbey mansion during the mid-18th century. The red-brick lodge occupies a site close to where a mill and tanyards existed during the 18th century. Until the mid-1960s hatches and eel traps existed where now can be seen the Queens Falls weir. In addition to the mill several buildings of quite large dimension existed here during the 18th century, adjacent to the river and the church, possibly part of the earlier monastic buildings complex.

The westerly end of Church Street, leading to Stonehenge Road, the cemetery and the recreation ground. The toll-house, the nearer of the two buildings, was demolished by a runaway vehicle in the late 1920's or early 1930's. The other building, Pink House cottage—or Little Thatch as it is currently named—still stands. It is interesting to note the line of the fencing which, until well into this century, ran at an angle to the road as it approached the river, a reminder of the way to the earlier ford and animal crossing. The boundary line has moved in more recent years to run parallel to the edge of the road.

The Great Bridge, otherwise Queensberry Bridge, from a 19th century engraving.

The title of Abbey is possessed today by the 19th century mansion and its surrounding parkland, the latter being much reduced from the acreage of former years. The parish church of St. Mary and St. Melor has also recently been restyled to become the Amesbury Abbey Church.

The abbey of today is in the private ownership of Sir Philip Antrobus, Baronet. It occupies the same site as its predecessors and some of the earliest monastic buildings. It is the later of two houses, the first having been built in 1660 by the architect John Webb, nephew and pupil of Inigo Jones, for the owner William Seymour the third duke of Somerset. Webb's house lasted for 173 years, having wings added during the mid 18th century and other more minor alterations undertaken at various other times.

The present mansion was built in 1834 for the then new owner Sir Edmund Antrobus. It consists of three storeys and attic executed in Chilmark stone, built around a central space with arcaded galleries on the first and second floors. It may not have been an entirely new building, but merely an enlargement and renovation of Webb's house. The self-taught architect, Thomas Hopper, continued the Palladian characteristics, intending the overall style to represent that of the earlier house. As originally conceived this present house had a sizeable ballroom along the south front and an imposing dining room in the 17th century style on the east side. Hopper was also able to take advantage of the modern technology of his time and incorporate large plate-glass windows into the design. The house today is divided into flats.

The Abbey Mansion in the early 19th century.

The Abbey Mansion today. The redesigned portico can be seen through the trees.

Existence of earlier monastic buildings on the same site was proven when, in 1860, excavations were made to the rear of the house for the purpose of adding servants' quarters. Wall and pillar footings, tiled flooring and other items of carved stonework were brought to light. Crop markings, noticed during the very dry summer of 1870 suggested the existence of further foundations to the east of the mansion, along the riverside towards Kent House. This tradition has never been substantiated and may only be evidence of the former 18th century formal gardens which are thought to have existed to the east of the house.

Examples of the varied design on the medieval floor tiles found in 1860.

Opposite the abbey entrance is a small lane, now known as Church Lane. It leads to, and was probably once part of, a footpath known as the Almanaze Path. This unusual name appears to be either a contraction of Almen (or Almond) Hayes, by which it was known in the mid 19th century, evolving from land held by the Hayes family who lived here in the 18th century, or by the access it gave to the Elm Hays field. The field at the end of Church Lane contained the October Fairs which were formerly held in the streets and earlier still in the churchyard.

The present vicarage was built about 1920. It stands a little to the east of the site of the earliest known vicarage which, until about 1888, stood just to the east of the church. It was widely assumed to have been the last of the remaining abbey buildings. At this time also cottages existed along what is now the vicarage wall. One was the home of the church sexton, Mr Joseph Spreadbury, during the latter part of the 19th century. Mr Spreadbury was unfortunately drowned while tending one of the hatches near Grey Bridge. During the period between these two vicarages, the Antrobus Arms served the purpose, prior to becoming an inn.

Across the road from the vicarage is the "Phoenix" cottage. Today the residence of the undertaker it was, at the turn of the century, a temperance hostel and restaurant frequented by cyclists. On the corner of this building can be seen a niche or chamfer cut into the corner by an earlier occupier, a shoemaker, to permit a view up the road. Next door to the Phoenix stood the Bear Inn, referred to as a coaching inn and noted for its fine oak panelling. It was destroyed by fire in 1870. The site houses the Dunkirk Veterans Club today, the building being the former church rooms and school. On the same side is the Antrobus Arms Hotel, formerly the Avon Temperance Hotel. The present building is much changed from the earlier Chopping Knife Inn which occupied the same site in the 18th century. The earlier character can be seen in the west wing adjoining the central hall and entrance. The blocked door, formerly for horse-drawn vehicles, suggests its original purpose. The east wing is of more recent construction, being formerly an open yard. Owned at one time by the local and well-known Pinckney family, it was sold to a Reverend Meyrick who, in 1868, made extensive alterations and additions to the inn which produced the present hotel, the adjoining parish rooms and the nearby house set back from the road called "Fairholme"—with its distinctive octagonal observatory—the whole combining to produce his residence and a school or college of noted reputation. It is recorded that teams from this school met those from Marlborough College on the Stonehenge cricket ground, reputedly the finest pitch in the county! On Sundays the scholars could be seen in their distinctive uniform of Eton jackets with silk toppers, escorted by their ushers clad in gowns and mortar-boards. It is, perhaps, a pity that Meyrick's school was so short-lived.

Church Street viewed from its eastern end at the turn of the century. Lloyds Bank now occupies the site where the gentleman stands in the doorway. The fine building across the road made way in 1970 for the present Abbey Square shopping precinct. Further down the road on the left is the King's Arms Inn and beyond that the vicarage which was to become the present Antrobus Arms Hotel.

Opposite the Antrobus Arms were cottages and gardens in the 18th century. More recently, when the vicarage and hotel car park were constructed, skeletons were found buried as if in a cemetery; possibly one connected with the monastic house. Skeletal remains feature in the former buildings on the adjoining premises also. Where the Abbey Square now stands, with its selection of modish shops, stood a fine 17th century red-brick house, with stone mullioned windows, leaded lights and distinctive chimney. This was, at the end of the 18th century, the residence of one Dr. Bloxham who, as an aid to his medical practice, kept a complete skeleton in a cupboard. The house was later divided into separate

The eastern end of Church Street at its junction with High Street and Salisbury Street. The major area of change between 1910 and the present day can be seen at the left in these two illustrations, where the thatched saddlery and haulier's dwelling provided the site in 1970 for the present shopping precinct.

dwellings occupied by a saddler's family who used the adjacent stable and coach house as a shop, and by the carrier who was also the postman. Around the mid 20th century the saddlery became an upholstery shop. Both of these buildings were demolished in 1971.

Opposite is the Kings Arms Inn, formerly named The Saracens Head. Although a building of early character and typical of many here that have long since gone, its use as an inn does not seem to have preceded the 18th century, being referred to in 1726 as a house, orchard and paddock belonging to a Mr Hays, the premises extending almost to Frog Lane (now Flower Lane). Earlier Amesbury historians have inferred its existence as an inn in 1763, when it is recorded by John Soul that, "the old Amesbury Friendly Society met here . . . " After the demise of the nearby market house, the inn was the meeting place of the courts Leet and Baron.

Between this building and Lloyds Bank on the corner of Church Street and Salisbury Street were shops and houses, the former exhibiting the bow window of which there now remains only one example, and this in Salisbury Street. The bank occupies approximately the site of the 18th century market house which stood in a commanding position at the north end of the market place, now Salisbury Street. The site was at the boundary of the Priory and Earldoms manors and the natural meeting place when both manors came under the one owner after the dissolution. The only surviving illustration of the market house suggests that the stocks—the machinery for punishment of local crimes—were also here, but this is not certain. It is known that they changed their position at various times. We are more certain that the public weighbridge was here, essential in later years for the assessment of tolls but even this moved to the south end of the market before it was rendered obsolete.

Having reached the market house, another convenient moment arises in which to pause and consider briefly its background and meaning to the local community as illustrated by the remaining accounts of the manorial court; for the market house was, in many ways, the focal point of communal life—it contained the weights and measures thus governing the standard of trade and was also the meeting place of the manorial court whilst it stood.

Manorial Life

As we have seen earlier Amesbury has evolved from a typical manorial system. Each class of person was kept very much in place by the manorial courts which made use of local unpaid officers. These courts—Courts Leet and Baron for Amesbury—concerned themselves with land holding and transfers, rents fines and services, common rules for cultivation and land management and the various rights of grazing, timber, fuel etc. The duties of each person were prescribed—to do service for the lord, to fight when required and to obey the seemingly complex but necessary system of farming and, last of all, to support himself and his family as best he could. Every action was regulated by the local court which was held in the market house every three weeks or so, and annually.

Intimate detail of life in Amesbury under its various manorial lords is scarce. All we have left now is one Book of Presentments of the Courts Leet and Baron for the Priory and Earldom Manors, which covers the period 1730 to 1854. The Court Leet concerned itself with minor infringements of the law, while the

Court Baron dealt with property and other territorial transactions. This remaining book of Presentments—earlier ones, thought to date from the 14th century, were consigned to fuel a fire within living memory—just lifts a corner of the curtain, giving a glimpse of the workings and life of manorial Amesbury.

With the one book we have left we can just see the workings of the manorial courts during their final period of decline, to the point where they became a legal formality, finally giving way to the onslaught of Victorian legislation and reform. The book was purchased by fifteen of the twenty jurymen who, with the two constables, two bailiffs, hayward, wayman and other officers, were elected annually. The initial entries reflect the importance of the courts to the local community. The Presentments begin by listing the rights and customs, the origins and fuller detail of which were long since lost; authority for an action being established by it being, " . . . according to the customs of the manor . . . " and as such the local tenant farmers were instructed:

The cows of ye Lord to go three days in each corne field before ye sheep.

A right for ye herd of cows of Great Amesbury to have three days feed in a little meadow called ye Butts and likewise in ye Little ffield after harvest before Mr. Haywards sheep.

Earls Farm flock of sheep to have no right of feed on Cuckold Hill and Townsend Field till 9 days before Michelmas.

The occupier of Countess Farm to have no way nor right of way to drive any manner of cattle through cowleas to lower leas from Ladyday to Martinstide . . .

. . . (has) a right way through New Leas to drive any manner of cattle to King's Island between Hollary Day and Martens Tide . . .

It is contrary to the customs of the manor to put any beasts into the Common before 3rd of May.

. . . contrary for horses to be put into the Common before Lammas.

. . . custom of this manor for the tennants who have a Right of Common to have a right to the shroud of trees standing thereon. Part of the Common field is enclosed near Parsonage Lane now in the occupation of William Warne. Occupiers of Countess Court Farm for enclosing part of the Common near Dark Lane throughing to another manor.

Having laid the ground rules to ensure that all things happened at an appointed time, the courts then had to ensure that the rules were obeyed. In this respect a certain Farmer Scanes receives particular attention:

. . . for allowing his ewes and lambs to feed on the Summer Field before St. Georges day.

. . . for putting more sheep on the Common than he was supposed to . . .

. . . for putting sheep in Martins Field against custom . . .

. . . for not putting a bull to the herd of beasts according to custom . . .

All this and more for Farmer Scanes, at only one meeting of the court. One might be tempted to feel sorry for him, except that he does appear as one of the elected jurors whose aim should perhaps have been to uphold and practise the rules, rather than to ignore them. Not a very good example to the 'ordinary man in the field'! His attitude does, however, help to illustrate the dwindling powers of the courts and of the manorial system during this period. No fines or punishments are recorded against his misdemeanours, it was already too futile an exercise to try and impose such penalties. The growing disillusionment felt by the ordinary

The Market House: demolished after a fire in 1809. A suggestion of stocks is visible at the far end.

person is perhaps shown by the entry for 17th October 1746, which records one, "... Asa Childs for breaking open the pound".

It was also the business of the courts to exercise authority in respect of the maintenance of territorial boundaries, the provision of standard weights and measures and the continuing good order of the various buildings in the community, all of which were owned by the lord. Hence we see the following typical entries:

Mr. Blatch the proprietor of Ratfyn Farm has encroached on the manor by plowing half the ditch between Ratfyn and Earls Farms. Mr. Hutchins has encroached on the manor by planting fir trees over the boundary between Porton and Red House Farms.

... the ditch in Great Boney Meadow should be cleared by the owner ...

John Osgood for ploughing 3 feet beyond his bounds near Salisbury Way.

Farmer Coster for hedging part of the Common near Shallow Water Meadow.

Mr. Poore and Mr. Pinckney for not keeping up the fence about Northam according to custom.

... Farmer Blake for breaking up a Linchet in South Mill Hill Field ...

The Pit at the great Elm to be very dangerous for people or cattle to fall into. The Pound ... and Stocks ... to be very much out of repair which is great deniance to the benefits of the tenants and ought to be repaired by the Lord of the said Manor.

... the Duke of Queensberry for causing part of a bank called Whitnam Bank to be carried away being part of the Common.

... the bound(ary) stalks in the field to be out of repair and the tenants desire that it should be done by the Lords of this Severall Manors.

... the Quart and Pint standard which was burnt and the weights and scales to be provided by His Grace.

These last entries help to give some idea of the responsibilities to be met by the head of the community. However, the number of times that the same entries appear in the court records before the action called for was completed gives an indication of the lack of interest felt by the duke of Queensberry towards the well-being of his village and people. The action of Asa Childs recorded above can, no doubt, be excused in the atmosphere of mounting frustration that must have existed.

Things could only improve. Eventually they did but not, apparently, until the estate came into the hands of Sir Edmund Antrobus in 1825. Among the entries during his period of ownership, it is recorded that a blindhouse was erected for the use of the town and a woodhouse was erected in Tanners Lane. A survey of the manorial boundaries was made in 1830, in the presence of Sir Edmund, after which about thirty men—presumably the jurors and other officers—dined at the New Inn. The remainder received bread, cheese and beer at the Kings Arms. The entry for the following year was very brief, " . . . We present all things well." This brevity is characteristic of the later entries, which concern themselves with the poor state of some of the roads—South Mill Hill being dangerous for carts and carriages and the turnpike near the churchyard being very narrow and dangerous for coaches. In 1843 John Harrison, the last hayward, was 'made redundant', his job being taken over by the relatively new rural police. The last notable entry appears in 1851 which says: "The footpath in Bakehouse Lane out of repair; likewise our manure heap."

High Street

Continuing our walk eastwards into the High Street we cross the Abbey Lane which once led directly from the market place into the priory grounds. In the 18th century this was lined with houses, barns and gardens. Remaining evidence of this earlier character can be seen in the portion of cob wall and in the brick and timber construction at the rear of the present newsagent and hardware shop. The importance of this part of Amesbury, as reflected in its buildings of superior architectural style, is also evident in the adjoining house and shop, currently a clothes and shoe shop.

Across the road from these premises is the former gaol, lock-up or blindhouse, situated on the corner of High Street and Salisbury Street. Erected in 1827, it replaces an earlier one incorporated in the abbey gatehouse, possibly Kent House. Its present role of estate agent's office allows it a little more decoration and fitting than would have been thought desirable for its original purpose, containing as it did two cells, each with its heavy iron studded door and grill. The character of the building has not confined it to those two uses; it has been a florist's, a motorcycle shop in the 1920s and, more lately, a milk bar and restaurant.

Next to the gaol in the High Street is a 17th or 18th century house standing now on what was given as "Church Land" in 1726. At present a hairdresser's establishment, it too has seen a variety of uses. Known at one time as Chimes House, it is recorded as being left as a legacy to the church by the mechanic who invented, installed and maintained the three-hour chimes in the church. The exact period in question is uncertain. Early in the 1920s it became the offices of the Amesbury Electric Light Company and later still, up to around the mid 1950s, it was the local wireless shop.

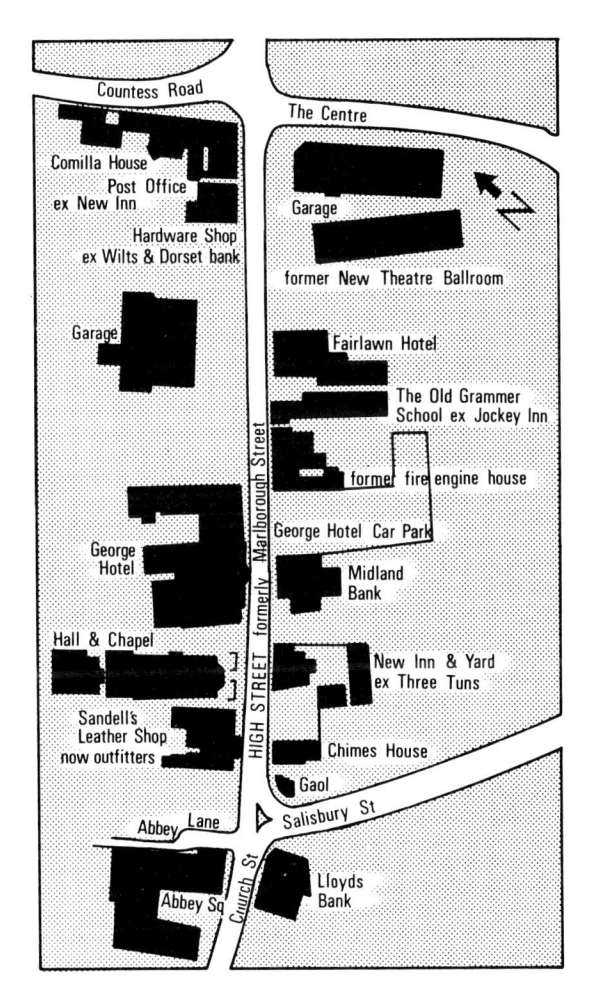

Next to Chimes House we have the New Inn and its car park. The rough chalk-block construction typical of this area can be clearly seen in the east wall. It is recorded in the 18th century as the Three Tuns Inn and Garden, run by one widow Vincent. The car-park, originally a tenement garden backing on to Marlborough Street (now High Street) became, around the turn of the century, the tanyard and works of the Sandell family, who continued a trade that had existed since the 14th century. Their shop was directly opposite. Across the road from the New Inn lies the Wesleyan Chapel. The present building, constructed in 1900, is the second on the site built to accommodate those who since the 17th century were described as Dissenters. The earlier chapel was built in 1838 and further enlarged in 1892. It was approached through a stone archway and would have been positioned behind the present chapel, the front portion of which occupies the site of a bakers' shop kept by the Misses Yarham who were noted for their lardy cakes and cooked ham.

Chimes House — once housed the offices of the electricity supply company and, in the illustration, is again seen at the centre of technological advance.

Next to the chapel is the George Hotel. The exact age and earlier history of this establishment are not certain. It is thought probable that it was connected with the abbey, permitting rest and refreshment to travellers, pilgrims and those on business with the abbey. The character of the present building is much changed from that of former years. In the 18th century it still retained the form of the traditional inn and hostelry, little changed from Medieval times; a rectangular structure, with central courtyard, approached by a curving drive leading off from the High Street. The west wing, added in the early 20th century occupies this area. Behind the main building were the stables, outhouses, gardens and orchards. This was the inn recorded by Dr Claver Morris in his "Diary of a West Country Physician" where, on the 5th and 6th of May 1721, he lodged whilst attending the horse fair at Stonehenge after enjoying a late breakfast of beef from the spit. In later years the George Hotel was the frequent venue for large meetings. It was here that the lord of the manor would provide the annual dinner for his tenants after the yearly rent audit; here also during the 19th century the Turnpike Trustees would occasionally meet and likewise the Board of Guardians until moving to their new workhouse premises. It was at one time the headquarters of the All-England Coursing Club and of the New Forest Coursing Club. Across the road from the hotel were its gardens, now a car-park. Next to this stands the Midland Bank. Prior to its construction the site contained the dwelling of William Cove Kemm, a brewer and publican and also a noted local historian. On the east side of the car-park are cottages of traditional rural character. The one nearest to the car-park, occupied in the 19th century by one Walton Soper, painter and parish clerk, later became the garage for the fire engine and, more recently a local taxi-driver's establishment. The adjoining cottage is now a greengrocer's. Across the road from these, adjoining the George Hotel, are the premises formerly occupied by the village's noted butcher and poulterer whose window display might almost defeat the efforts of his modern counterparts! Although that business ceased around the mid-20th century and the shop has since been the home of various diverse activities, it still retains some of the tile-work that provided the elegant facade during its original period of use. The cattle pens and slaughter-house have long since disappeared or been absorbed into alternative activities.

Next to these premises now stands a line of shops where formerly stood houses and gardens; then comes one of the two earliest garages in Amesbury. This is also the site of Asa Childs' residence, who we saw earlier had his own ideas of local justice when his animals were impounded! It is thought that the garage site, or the immediate vicinity, was the location of the Gauntlet pipe factory from the number of bowls and stems that have been recovered here from time to time.

The former gaol at the corner of Salisbury Street and High Street. Later becoming a florist's, motor cycle retailer, milk-bar and currently estate agent. What next. . . . ?

The earliest available photograph of the High Street. Taken towards the end of the 19th century it shows, on the left, Sally Yarham's cake shop and the Stonehenge Temperance Hotel where now stands the Methodist chapel built in 1900. At the time of the photograph the chapel existed to the rear of the shops and was approached through the archway.

The High Street around 1915. The addition of street lighting and the evident transition from horse-drawn to motor transport marks the beginning of a much wider change.

By the 1930's the change was much advanced and a new maturity evident. The new west wing of the George Hotel was already ivy-covered. Less attractive were the electricity supply and telegraph posts.

Even today the fundamental structure of the street remains more or less intact, only the embellishments change.

Opposite Sloan's garage is the former Rose's Charity Grammar School. It is of superior traditional construction, with neatly squared and laid chalk blocks, contrasting with the less elegant construction with the same medium in adjacent buildings. This school, probably of 17th century origin, has seen a variety of uses. In 1726 it appears as the White Hart Inn and Gardens of Anthony Cook Kenton. Later that century it had become the Jockey Inn, with stables; it was the subject of a fire in 1751. In 1807 it became a schoolmaster's residence and grammar school, fulfilling as well the function of post office during the latter part of the 19th century. Its function as a school ceased in 1899 since when it has been a private residence.

Next door is the Fairlawn Hotel. Built in the latter part of the 19th century and formerly with coach-house, stables and a yard, it was earlier known as Fovant House, the residence of Mr George Best Batho the surgeon. There were two adjoining premises, the first—again with stables, coach-house and gardens— was known as Fair Lawn and was occupied during the 19th century by a Doctor Charles Pyle who, in addition to his medical practice seems to have run some sort of finishing school for young ladies. The other building was a cottage, entered via two stone steps and was the sweet-shop of Widow Eyres. These premises were more recently a cafe which retained the Fairlawn name, and have subsequently become small antique and audio shops. The remainder of this side of the High Street to the junction with the A345 contains now a recently derelict garage premises of interesting and characteristic 1930s architectural style. The site has now been re-vitalised by the other of Amesbury's two oldest garage businesses. This frontage to the High Street was formerly occupied by Robinson's the chemist and William Hough, a noted watch and clock maker. Until the mid 1950s the site also contained the New Theatre Ballroom, billed as the largest dance hall in the south-west. It featured groups, bands and many celebrity names.

1914: troubled times, and Amesbury's National Reserves prepare.

Displays such as in this High Street shop between the wars are now a rarity.

The present post-office—formerly the New Inn.

High Street from its easterly end. The building in the right foreground now houses the much travelled post-office, whilst that of the undertaker on the left of the picture is now a garage forecourt.

The present day, where character is beginning to give way to commerce.

On the opposite side of the road there now stands the Post Office with toy shop and stationers, housed in one of Amesbury's older and more interesting buildings which has seen a variety of uses. An adjoining hardware shop in imitation architectural style started life as a coach-house, and later fulfilled the function of Wilts and Dorset Bank. It is the Post Office on the corner that merits close attention.

Examination of the outside reveals some interesting characteristics. The stone blocks forming the chequer work contain some of green sandstone, a material foreign to this area. It is unlikely that this stone would have been used from choice, unless available from a local source. It is probable therefore that this greenstone came from the demolished abbey buildings as such material was included among that sold to local people. Further possible evidence of this source of building material can be seen in the fragments of carved stonework visible on the High Street side. The corbel just under the eaves at the corner of the building, whilst also from the abbey, was placed in its present position some years ago by the owner of the building. In 1726 this establishment, with the adjoining Comilla House just around the corner, is given as the New Inn, house and gardens of William Stallard. It appears likely that the house fulfilled much the same function from the early 17th century as, in the Lenten Recognisances, one Agnes Matravers, tippler, agreed not to permit meat to be prepared or sold in her house during Lent, or on any Friday. She is also given as the occupier of the house at the north-east corner of the High Street in the manorial perambulation of 1639. The premises may have been operating as an inn as late as 1829. It was certainly remembered as such in that year when William Wiltshire the butcher was killed when his cart overturned after hitting the wall of this building "at great speed". This location was evidently even then an accident black spot, as William Wiltshire was not the only person to meet his doom there, a man called Hicks meeting a similar fate a few years before.

The Centre

Turning right at the east end of the High Street on arrives at the Centre, which replaces the earlier School Lane or Back Lane, on the west side, close to the junction with High Street were 18th century houses and yards. Later, into the 20th century, a timber yard, or pimp yard, existed on the corner providing kindling wood. A carpenter's shop and saw pits were also here and a pile of huge tree trunks for cutting into timber was a common sight. This area later became a taxi stand. A little further along, still in the present garage premises, a house and farm buildings were destroyed by fire in 1809, being replaced at a later date by a grain mill and store. This site eventually became a County Council depot until around the 1950's ending up, as at present, a garage yard.

Opposite this, where another petrol station flourishes today, stood a draper's shop and dwelling owned, at the turn of the century, by Frank Tucker. When his business moved to Salisbury Street the premises became one of the varied sites of a motorcycle shop. By the second world war period the buildings had been demolished, the area being just waste ground and waiting for the next development.

Proceeding southwards along the Centre towards Kitchener Road, one passes

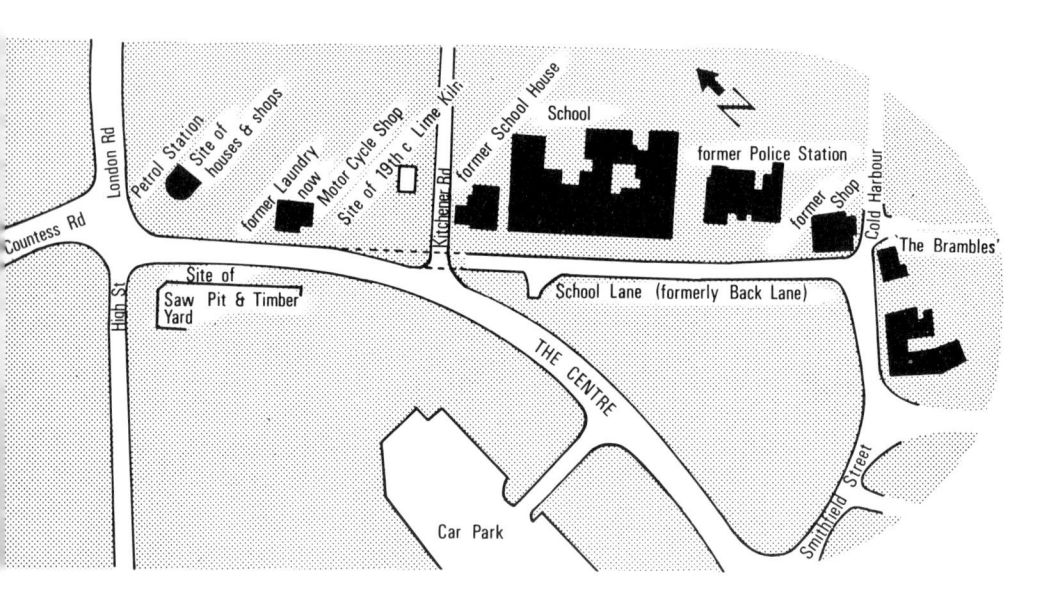

Map labels:
- Countess Rd
- London Rd
- High St
- Petrol Station
- Site of houses & shops
- former Laundry now Motor Cycle Shop
- Site of 19th c. Lime Kiln
- Kitchener Rd
- former School House
- School
- former Police Station
- former Shop
- Cold Harbour
- 'The Brambles'
- Site of Saw Pit & Timber Yard
- School Lane (formerly Back Lane)
- THE CENTRE
- Car Park
- Smithfield Street

the present motorcycle shop which utilises the former laundry premises. Next to this, the private house occupies the 19th century site of the lime kiln. Then, Kitchener Road. Presumably named for the usual patriotic reasons and the fact that the presence of the Army had made such a difference to the village economy, it has only relatively recently been hard-surfaced. Prior to this, in the 1940s, it was only a rough track leading to pigsties and Crooked Covert Copse. Its line corresponds with an 18th century boundary between two holdings in Town's End Little Field.

After Kitchener Road we have the school house, school and former police station all built along the edge of the same field. Although now possessing various architectural additions and subtractions this group of buildings still shows the attempt to produce an example of co-ordinated civic construction of the Edwardian era. The school, built in 1901, brought together the earlier diverse charity and private educational establishments under the control of the Parish Church. The police station, which later became the divisional headquarters, allowed for the more efficient operation of the County Police which had been formed since 1839, and replaced the former police station, now demolished, in Salisbury Street, and its associated lock-up. At the South End of School Lane is the entrance to Coldharbour. Facing the end of the lane is one of the three remaining thatched roofs which, with the house on the opposite corner, give a good idea of the earlier character that existed among these modern dwellings.

The junction of High Street, London Road, Countess Road and the Centre, as it appears today. Comilla House, part of the former New Inn, is on the right.

The scene from a similar viewpoint around 1910. Frank Tucker's drapers shop at the left has become a petrol station, whilst the timber yard and grain store at the right is now a car sales forecourt.

The same junction in 1939. Frank Tucker's shop had become Bugdens Motor Cycle Depot before being finally demolished in the early 1940's

A view of the same junction looking north. Countess Road leads away to the left and the trees of Lords Walk are in the background.

A view along present-day School Lane, formerly Back Lane.

Smithfield Street

Turning right from School Lane one enters Smithfield Street. Its name implies a former use as a cattle market or fair place. This is substantiated by a recorded memory that Smithfield Street and Bakehouse Lane were remembered as being ful of horses and cattle at an annual fair. Such an event would have been served by the Greyhound Inn, referred to by this name as long ago as 1740 when it was observed by the manorial court to be out of repair.

Opposite the Greyhound is the recently constructed health centre and library complex which occupies the former site of Amesbury House, an early 19th century house in which the Antrobus family are supposed to have resided when first coming to the village.

Crossing Earls Court Road, formerly Bakers or Bakehouse Lane, situated at the north end of the present line of shops—the Arcade—is the former library premises. Built originally to house the village fire engine early this century, it has just become a baker's premises. At the other side of the adjacent Edwards Road, so named to remind us of Job Edwards, one of Amesbury's noted earlier historians, is the cinema. The background to this amenity is worth considering in a little more detail.

The cinema is situated on part of the site of the former Ivydene guest-house which was burned down in 1911. No sooner had this disaster occurred than the site, which includes the present Co-operative stores, became occupied by the travelling bioscope. It arrived pulled by an enormous steam tractor called "Pride of the South" and took the form of three large trailers which, when unpacked became stage, screen and projection area, the whole being assembled and contained under canvas. It stood more or less where the present cinema stands. With dancers and organ to provide supplementary attractions the bioscope must have made a major impact upon this still closely-knit little community, attracting even those from Salisbury, whose similar cinematographic establishments it is thought to have preceded. The canvas top was eventually succeeded by a more permanent wooden building which after a while itself proved unsuited to cope with the large audiences that were attracted to the shows. The cinema was moved temporarily to the present site of Pitts Garage, next to the bus station. In 1936 the magnificent modern edifice was constructed and opened by Miss Betty Fields, Gracie's sister. The new cinema, however, even with its modern brick construction in the art-deco style and its improved comfort lacked the air of rural informality of its forerunner. The occasional collapse of a row of seats in later years was no match for the days of silent films when the delight of the audience was not solely confined to the actions displayed on the screen but also included close attention to the manual dexterity of the person operating the sound effects and showing ribald appreciation when those effects failed to coincide with the actions they were meant to help illustrate.

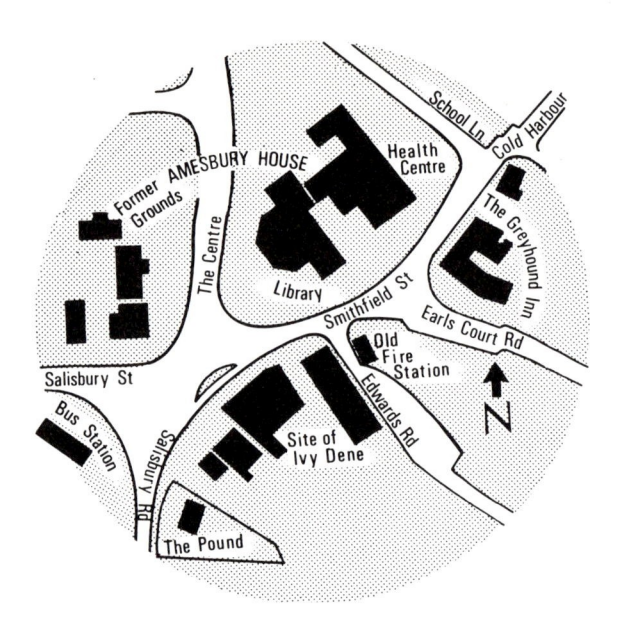

Returning to the pre-cinema era, Ivydene was a thatched guesthouse with adjacent malthouse containing wooden lattice windows, which was approached via massive gates with pillars. It was the residence, in the mid 19th century, of Job Edwards, the local maltster and antiquarian. Its destruction by fire was a fate met by so many of the village's buildings; the fire removing what was probably a building of major importance to the character of central Amesbury, allowing, once it had gone, the beginning of the new wave of architectural development. The Ivydene fire was undoubtedly the first great test of the 22-man manual fire engine purchased by the Amesbury Fire Brigade Committee

Smithfield Street and the entrance to Coldharbour just after 1900. The Greyhound Inn appears at the extreme right.

The same view today.

115

The Ivydene guest house was a dominant feature of the village central area. The remaining patch of grass was once a larger village green.

Immediately after the burning of Ivydene in 1911 the first permanent cinema appeared. Here, the ruins of Ivydene are hidden by the cinema hoardings behind the war memorial. The cinema itself is just to the left. To the left of the war memorial is the young chestnut tree planted to commemorate the coronation of George V.

The present character of the central area was becoming established in the 1930's with the arrival of the Co-operative store on the Ivydene site.

The chestnut tree, now well on its way to maturity, hides the Co-op and the newly erected Plaza cinema in this late 1930's scene. To the right, the forecourt of the Wilts and Dorset bus station replaces the cob wall visible in earlier pictures.

The present day. War memorial, chestnut tree and green have all gone, replaced by a complex and unsightly array of road signs and markings.

Amesbury House, viewed here from the north, was demolished to make way for the library and health centre in the late 1960's.

118

as one of its first actions when formed in 1902. If people have a mind to complain about today's fire service, let them think how the owners of Ivydene must have felt, waiting with bucket in hand whilst horses were rounded up in the field at the bottom of Coldharbour, led to the engine-house in the High Street and harnessed up to eventually rush to the scene. Providing there was sufficient hose to reach the river and enough strong men, the action could then commence! The distance from the river proved problematical in the Ivydene case, requiring the additional assistance of the Salisbury Fire Brigade, the Artillery brigade from Bulford and help from employees of the Bristol Aeroplane Company at Larkhill. Such was the gravity of these occasions that the help of everyone was welcomed, passers-by, hotel residents, locals and the vicar. It was also noted in contemporary accounts that certain idle local persons would not assist in manning the engine but were happy to just stand by and watch the action!

The last remaining evidence of Ivydene and its 19th century owner was a little summerhouse positioned in the corner of the yard behind the present Co-operative store. This summerhouse was built with surplus material from the church restorations of 1852. It was pulled down in the early 1970s, the materials disposed of and another link with old Amesbury and its history lost.

The house next to the Co-op, known earlier as Merchant's cottage and presently the dentist's surgery, was one of the sites of the nomadic post-office which moved here during the latter part of the 19th century from "Ye Olde Shoppe" in Salisbury Street. References to the Merchant family occur in the 1639 perambulation. Adjoining this are the former business premises and timber yard of William Bishop, the local builder, undertaker, mason and general handyman around the turn of the century. This family is also well established in the history of the village, earlier members being elected jurors to the manorial court in the 18th and 19th centuries.

Bishop's timber yard abutted onto another of the few but important former public facilities, the Pound. Its purpose was to contain such livestock that had strayed, caused damage or was not readily identifiable until the owner could be traced and made to pay the fine incurred for the damages or whatever involved. The original structure is, of course, no longer visible but the name lives on with the present house on the site. Opposite the Pound were cob-walled cottages where now the brick wall stands feebly attempting to hide huge lorries.

Flower Lane

We will wend our way round to Salisbury Street the long way, via Flower Lane. Continuing past the Pound we reach the junction of Salisbury Road and Flower Lane, this portion of which was formerly called Tanners Lane, presumably a reminder of a craft that was practised here prior to the 18th century. On the north side of the entrance the three cottages remind one of the older character of the area, although these cottages have lost their thatched roofs. On the south side of the entrance the seed merchant's replaces an earlier wheelwright's premises. An extremely large lime tree, felled in the early part of the century, is remembered in the cottage name. Whilst here, we can also spend a minute considering the fire station even though it is, strictly speaking, situated in Salisbury Road.

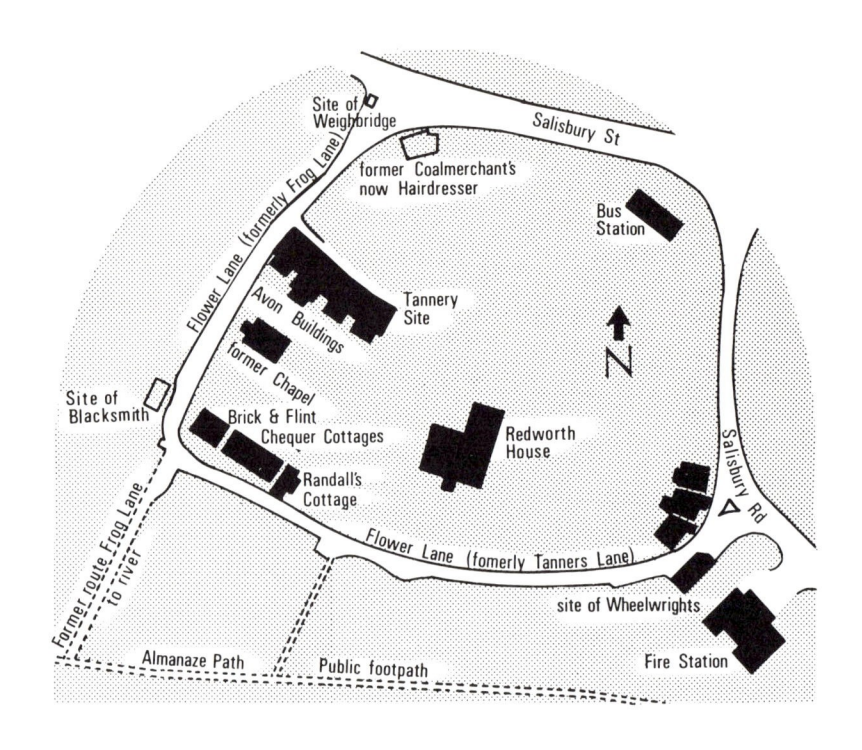

Felling the lime tree in Flower Lane. Occasions like this were always guaranteed to draw a crowd.

120

The first motorised fire engine, a Daimler, acquired around 1920.

The second fire engine, a Dennis, and its brigade just before the second world war.

As we saw earlier, the Fire Brigade Committee was formed at the beginning of the 20th century and acquired a manual engine. Prior to this, the only equipment available to fight fires was the engine invented by the Reverend Thomas Holland and such ladders and hooks that might be available to pull thatch from burning roofs. Hence the acquisition of the manual engine used at Ivydene was a considerable advance. Another major step forward occurred a little later, possibly around 1920, with the arrival of a motorised engine. Housed in its new garage next to the cinema, its presence helped the villagers to sleep much more soundly in their beds! In 1938 responsibility for the fire brigade passed to the Rural District Council, becoming nationalised in 1942. In 1947 it came under the influence of the Fire Services Act and from that time has been run by the County Council as fire authority. The present accommodation for the now much enlarged fire brigade was constructed in the early 1950s.

Continuing on round Flower Lane, one arrives at Redworth House. This 19th century building was the residence of a prosperous builder named Quint Cole. It later became the meeting place of the Amesbury Rural District Council and is now used mainly by the Social Services Department of the County Council. The village manure heap, referred to earlier, was also here at the corner of the grounds. Passing hastily on from that site one reaches a cottage abutting onto the lane. It was, at the beginning of the 20th century, the residence of one Edward Randall, a noted glove and breeches maker, whose additional responsibilities as verger extended to ringing the "death bell" at the passing of his fellow villagers.

Next to this dwelling is a row of attractive early 19th century cottages in chequer stone and flint. These are situated at the former junction of Tanners Lane and Frog Lane, the latter being the part that runs east-west from the river up to Salisbury Street. Turning the corner into "Frog Lane" there was, at the beginning of the 20th century, a blacksmith's premises where now exists the entrance to the GPO. exchange. Across the way is a former Primitive Methodist chapel, constructed from corrugated iron sheet and painted green. No-one is quite sure when it was last used as a chapel or by what denomination but general opinion suggests that it fulfilled its original purpose until the early part of the 20th century. From here up to Salisbury Street the character of Flower Lane has altered appreciably since the 1950s. The red-brick dwellings remaining give a good idea of the former character. Avon Buildings, for instance, are on the site of former tanyards according to local tradition. This may account for the wool warehouse or store that existed in front of Avon Buildings at the turn of the century. It was replaced by dwellings and shops, which in turn were demolished at least ten years ago, apparently to make way for a less than desirable empty space which may, in the near future, be transformed into a garden centre. The hairdresser's establishment at the south corner of Flower Lane and Salisbury Street replaces an earlier thatched dwelling and coal merchant's premises. On the opposite side the weighbridge existed during the early years of this century until becoming obsolete, the facility being removed to the east end of the village. Here also one could have seen another product of local talent, one Joe "Boneser" the contortionist. He lived in a caravan near to the tollhouse in Stonehenge Road but his "pitch" was at the end of Flower Lane, where he would delight youngsters with exhibitions of his skill in fire-eating and glass-eating. And so, by a devious route, we find ourselves in Salisbury Street.

Salisbury Street

If the north end of Salisbury Street, with its market house, manorial court and close proximity to the abbey, was the focal point of the village, then the south end of the street achieved a balance by its equally important commercial activities of trading and the cattle and horse fairs, bringing together the people from outlying villages to the south and east over the downs along Edmiston Road, Allington Road, Newton-Toney Road, the Durnford Path and West-Amesbury Wood-way, all of which, in the 18th century, converged on Bakehouse Lane and South Mill Lane and from these on to the Market Place, now Salisbury Street.

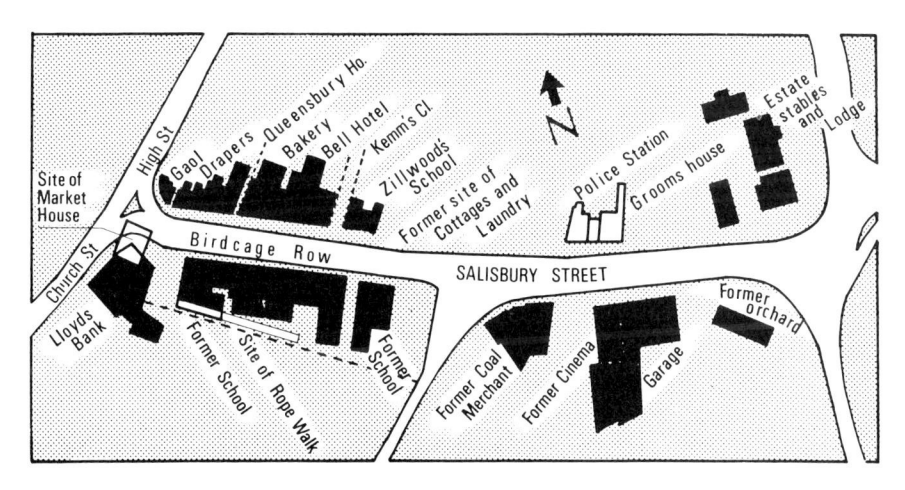

Salisbury Street viewed from the south-east end, prior to 1920. At this time the public weighbridge was situated at the entrance to Flower Lane, to the left and behind the group of children.

Salisbury Street viewed from the north-west end at the time of the first world war.

A similar view today.

124

The south-east end of the street. The picturesque cottages were demolished to make way for a garage premises which has itself been recently demolished for a new supermarket development.

The earliest impression we can gain of the market place is from the early 18th century and at that time it was a very different place from that of today. It possessed all the traditional character expected of such an important part of the village. The street was twice the width of the present road, with large mature trees along its centre. It was bounded on the west with orchards and gardens and a rope-walk where now exists "Birdcage Row" with its butcher, greengrocer, chemist and cafe; formerly with schools at either end, that at the south being the National Infants School, the older children attending the school at the north end of the row. This latter establishment later became a garage during the early 20th century, followed by use as a grocery and currently a cafe.

The east side of the market was built up with houses, closes and the hostelry very necessary for the proper conduct of market affairs. Today a great deal of this character has been lost. The southern end of Salisbury Street is, generally, a hotch-potch of inferior utilitarian architecture, with bus station, garages and council depot, but the north end still retains a semblance of its former self.

One redeeming feature of the south end is the former gate-house and stables of the now vanished Amesbury House. Derelict for some time and in danger of demolition, these 19th-century buildings are being developed and restored by a local company, to become an attractive central town house site. The cottage possesses the last hand water pump in the village.

Mid-way along the east side of Salisbury Street, the present Bell Inn, built around the 1920s, replaces an earlier establishment of the same name, which was recorded as existing in 1880. This in turn was apparently constructed on the site of the collapsed residence in the tenancy of one Philpot, which may have been the Swan Inn, noted as being handy for the market in the mid-18th century and known to have existed during the 17th century.

During the first quarter of this century an alleyway called Kemm's Square led along the side of the present Bell Inn to private dwellings. Another similar alley existed a little further along, next to Ye Olde Shoppe. This one has been infilled with what is currently an hairdresser's establishment.

Next to the Bell, and opposite the former infants school, was another similar establishment run by the Zillwood family in the 19th century; it is currently an estate agent's premises. Proceeding northwards from the Bell, the buildings display quite clearly their early character. They form a pleasing group of bakery, dwelling (formerly Queensberry Hotel) and draper's. The bakery is thought to date from the 16th century in parts, and once contained a fireplace that was thought to have originated in the abbey.

In Conclusion

From what we have seen on this survey it is clear that the village has experienced an intensive period of change over the last hundred years. Not all of the change has been for the general good. Most has been for commercial gain, the result of which has left some permanent scars, sweeping away traditional buildings that have stood the test of time and have helped to form a distinctive village character over many centuries. For example, from a village once exhibiting a predominance of thatched roofs we now have only three remaining. These traditional buildings have been replaced by purpose-built architecture, the least requirement of which is that it should blend harmoniously with its surroundings. There is currently a faintly detectable mood suggesting that the local people and the local authorities are once again taking more than just a passing interest in the character of the village. Let us hope that vision, where it counts, can capture such traditional character that still remains and blend with it the new, before it is too late.

NOTES AND SOURCES

Chapter One

Principal sources for the whole of chapter one are: the sites and monuments record maintained by Wiltshire Library & Museum Service at their Trowbridge headquarters; also the two parts of the *Victoria History of Wiltshire*, volume one.
    The First Inhabitants   General sources: Stone, 1958; Grinsell, 1958; Atkinson, 1956.
    Vespasian's Camp   General sources: Cunliffe, 1974; Forde-Johnston, 1976; Hogg, 1975; Webster and Dudley, 1973. Vespasian's campaign: Branigan, 1973.
    Saxon Amesbury before the Abbey   Earl's Farm Down villa: Cunnington, 1930–2; Hillfort reoccupation: Fowler, 1971; Morris, 1973; Place-names: Gover, *et al*, 1939; Mawer and Stenton, 1927; London Road excavation: Kemm, 1970.

Chapter Two

See, for the whole of chapter two, Pugh, 1956.
    The Foundation of the Abbey   General source: Stenton, 1971; St. Melor: Chandler, 1978.
    Domesday Amesbury   Royal estate: Barlow, 1970; Domesday survey: Darlington, 1955; Town development: Pugh, 1947–8; Hinton, 1977; Watermills: Gimpel, 1976.
    The End of the First Abbey   General source: Knowles, 1963; Amesbury: Kite, 1899–1901.

Chapter Three

For the whole of this chapter the following should be consulted: Pugh, 1956; Pugh, 1947–8; Pugh, 1947.
    The Priory   Chettle, 1942; Pevsner, 1975; Kemm, W. C. quoted by Ruddle in *Devizes Gazette*, 3.8.1899 (W. A. S. Cuttings File, 7, 231).
    Pilgrims and Legends   Chandler, 1978.
    Medieval Town   Notes: 1. Pugh, 1947, no. 100; 2. Pugh, 1947, no. 15; 3. Pugh, 1978, no. 788; 4. Pugh, 1947, no. 32; 5. Pugh, 1947, no. 75; 6. Pugh, 1947, no. 96; 7. Pugh, 1947, no. 67, dated 1474 is the earliest reference; 8. Salisbury Diocesan Record Office, Dissenters Meeting House Certificates, 31.10.1816; 9. Pugh, 1947, no. 63; 10. Pugh, 1947, nos. 9, 15; 11. Pugh, 1947, no. 67. Sources: Scott, 1959; Beresford, 1959; Pugh, 1978.
    The Dissolution   Youings, 1972.

Chapter Four

The Squire   Edwards, 1876; Moore, 1976; see also Wiltshire Record Office, 377/4 and W. A. S. Cuttings File, 1, 356.

The Tenants   This account is based largely on the census enumerator's returns for 1851, microfilm copy in the Wiltshire Record Office (Amesbury is on reel 19). Additional information derived from Kemm, 1970, the Amesbury Tithe award and map (Wiltshire Record Office) and local directories.

Agriculture   Notes: 1. Pugh, 1947, no. 78; 2. Pugh, 1947, nos. 130, 151; 3. Wiltshire Record Office, 283/6: Amesbury survey of 1742; 4. Wiltshire Record Office, 944/3: Field book and plan; 5. Wiltshire Record Office, 283/202. Sources: Pugh, 1947; Kemm, 1970; Hobsbawm and Rude, 1969; Bettey, 1977; Cobbett, 1830 (quotations are from the Nelson edition, pp. 342, 346).

Chapter Five

The Clay Pipe Industry   Aubrey, 1847; Fuller, 1952; Stevens, 1882; Ruddle, 1893–5; Atkinson, 1965; Atkinson, 1970; Atkinson, 1972; Oswald, 1975; Brown, 1959.

Turnpikes and Stagecoaches   Chandler, 1979.

Shopkeepers and Tradesmen   Markets and fairs: Pugh, 1947; Kemm, 1970; Bettey, 1977; Shopkeepers: local directories, 1793–1911.

Chapter Six

Poverty   Note: 1. Wiltshire Record Office, 377/4, letter 5.3.1792. Sources: General: Webb, 1929; Bagley, 1966; Specific: Goodhugh, 1970; Lewis, 1957.

Fires   1714 (West Amesbury): W. A. S. Cuttings File, 7, 224; 1745: Kemm, 1970; W. A. S. Cuttings File, 7, 224; 1751: Kemm, 1970; W. A. S. Cuttings File, 7, 224; 14, 222; 1761: W. A. S. Cuttings File, 26, 33; 1803: Kemm, 1970; W. A. S. Cuttings File, 7, 224; 1848: Kemm, 1970; W. A. S. Cuttings File, 7, 224; 1899 (July 21st): W. A. S. Cuttings File, 7, 376; 12, 54; 14, 222; 1899 (October 31st): W. A. S. Cuttings File, 7, 376; 1911: W. A. S. Cuttings, 13, 128.

Religion   General: *Victoria History of Wiltshire*, volume three; Thomas Holland: Willoughby, 1971; Fowle: a collection of printed sermons at Salisbury Reference Library; Early nonconformity: Turner, 1911; Unpublished sources: Salisbury Diocesan Record Office, churchwardens presentments, 1662, 1683, Returns to visitation queries, 1783, 1864, 1867, 1870, Return of certified places of worship, 1852, Meeting-house certificates (indexed); Wiltshire Record Office, meeting-house certificate 26.9.1719; Dr. Williams Library, John Evans list of dissenting congregations, 1715–1729. Wesley: Wesley, 1909.

Education   Endowed charities *(County of Wilts) return*, parish of Amesbury, 1905; Kemm, 1970; local directories; Salisbury Diocesan Record Office, returns to visitation queries, 1864, 1867, 1870.

Into the Twentieth Century   Army: Parker, 1977; Clarke-Smith, 1975; Railways: Moon, 1977; Thody, 1974.

BIBLIOGRAPHY

This bibliography includes the principal published sources for the history of the parish of Amesbury (excluding Stonehenge), as well as a number of more general works which have been used in the preparation of this book.

Amesbury district plan: report of studies, Salisbury: Salisbury District Council, 1975
Antrobus, F. C. M., *A Sentimental and practical guide to Amesbury and Stonehenge*, Amesbury: Amesbury Estate Office, revised edition, N.D. (c. 1908)
Atkinson, D. R., 'Clay tobacco pipes and pipemakers of Marlborough,' in *Wiltshire Archaeological Magazine* lx (1965), pp. 85–96
Atkinson, D. R. 'Clay tobacco pipes and pipemakers of Salisbury, Wiltshire,' in *Wiltshire Archaeological Magazine* lxv (1970), pp. 177–189
Atkinson, D. R., 'Further notes on clay tobacco pipes and pipemakers from the Marlborough and Salisbury districts,' in *Wiltshire Archaeological Magazine* lxvii (1972), pp. 149–156
Atkinson, R. J. C., *Stonehenge*, London: Hamish Hamilton, 1956
Aubrey, J., *The Natural history of Wiltshire* . . . , London: Wiltshire Topographical Society, 1847
Backinsell, W. G. C., *The Medieval clock in Amesbury Abbey*, Salisbury: South Wiltshire Industrial Archaeology Society, 1979 (SWIAS Historical Monograph Series 3)
Bagley, J. J. & A. J., *The English poor law*, London: Macmillan, 1966
Barlow, F., *Edward the Confessor*, London: Eyre & Spottiswoode, 1970
Beresford, M. W., 'Fifteenths and tenths: quotas of 1334,' and 'Poll-tax payers of 1377,' in *Victoria History of Wiltshire* iv (1959), pp. 294–313
Bettey, J. H., *Rural life in Wessex 1500–1900*, Bradford-on-Avon: Moonraker Press, 1977
Birch, S., *The Abbey of Ambresbury: a poem*, London: T. Cadell *et al.*, 2 parts, 1788–1789
Brakspear, H., 'On "the Jessye" at Amesbury,' in *Wiltshire Notes and Queries* iii (1899–1901), pp. 366–368
Branigan, K., 'Vespasian in the south-west', in *Proceedings of the Dorset Natural History and Archaeological Society* xcv (1973), pp. 50–57
Brown, W. E., 'Tobacco and clay pipes,' in *Victoria History of Wiltshire* iv (1959), pp. 240–244
Chandler, J. H., 'Three Amesbury legends,' in *Hatcher Review* vi (1978), pp. 12–23
Chandler, J. H., *The Amesbury Turnpike Trust*, Salisbury: South Wiltshire Industrial Archaeology Society, 1979 (SWIAS. Historical Monograph Series 4)
Chandler, J. H., (ed.) *The Amesbury Millennium lectures*, Trowbridge: Wiltshire County Council, forthcoming
Chettle, H. F., 'The English houses of the order of Fontevraud,' in *Downside Review* lxx (1942), pp. 33–55
Clarke-Smith, E., 'Salisbury Plain,' in *The Tidworth guide: an information handbook and directory*, Gloucester: British Publishing Co., N. D. (1975), pp. 65–85
Clifford, H. D., 'Where medieval nuns resided,' in *Country Life* cxxviii (1.9.1960), pp. 442–443

Cobbett, W., *Rural rides*, London: Nelson, N. D. (first published 1830)
Cunliffe, B., *Iron age communities in Britain*, London: Routledge & Kegan Paul, 1974
Cunnington, M. E., 'Romano-British Wiltshire . . . ,' in *Wiltshire Archaeological Magazine* xlv (1930–1932), pp. 166–216
Darlington, R. R., 'Translation of the text of the Wiltshire Domesday,' in *Victoria History of Wiltshire* ii (1955), pp. 113–168
Dufty, A. R., 'Amesbury Church,' in *Archaeological Journal* civ (1947), pp. 156–158
Edwards, J., *Amesbury gleanings: chiefly in reference to the association of the families of Seymour and Douglas with that place*, (Salisbury): W. A. & N. H. S. Local Committee, 1876
Field, J., *English field-names*, Newton Abbot: David & Charles, 1972
Forde-Johnston, J., *Hill forts of the iron age in England and Wales: a survey of the surface evidence*, Liverpool: Liverpool Univ. Press, 1976
Fowler, P. J., 'Hill-forts, AD. 400–700,' in Hill, D. & Jesson, M., (eds.) *The Iron age and its hill-forts . . .* , Southampton: Southampton Univ. Archaeological Society, 1971, pp. 203–213
Fuller, T., *The Worthies of England*, edited . . . by John Freeman, London: Allen & Unwin, 1952
Gimpel, J., *The Medieval machine: the industrial revolution of the middle ages*, London: Gollancz, 1976
Godfrey, J., *The Church in Anglo-Saxon England*, Cambridge: Cambridge Univ. Press, 1962
Goodhugh, P. S., 'The Poor law in Amesbury,' in *Wiltshire Industrial Archaeology* ii (1970), pp. 6–12
Gover, J. E. B., Mawer, A., & Stenton, F. M., *The Place-names of Wiltshire*, Cambridge: Cambridge Univ. Press, 1939 (English Place-Name Society, vol. 16)
Grinsell, L. V., *The Archaeology of Wessex*, London: Methuen, 1958
Guthrie, J. G. S., (ed.) *What to see in and around Amesbury and Stonehenge*, Salisbury: Salisbury District Council, N. D. (1977)
Hinton, D. A., *Alfred's kingdom: Wessex and the south 800–1500*, London: Dent, 1977 (History in the Landscape series)
Hoare, Sir R. Colt, *The History of modern Wiltshire: Hundreds of Everley, Ambresbury, and Underditch*, London: John Nichols & Son, 1826 (Modern History of South Wiltshire, vol. 2, part 2)
Hobsbawm, E. J., & Rude, G., *Captain Swing*, (London): Lawrence & Wishart, 1969
Hogg, A. H. A., *Hill-forts of Britain*, London: Hart-Davis, 1975
Hoskins, W. G., *Local history in England*, London: Longman, 2nd edition, 1973
Hughes, G. W. G., 'Notes on the courts leet and baron in Amesbury, Wilts.,' in *Wiltshire Archaeological Magazine* xlvii (1937), pp. 521–525
Jackson, J. E. 'Ambresbury monastery,' in *Wiltshire Archaeological Magazine* x (1867), pp. 61–84
Jaggard, W. R., *Experimental Cottages: a report on the work of the department at Amesbury, Wiltshire*, London: H.M.S.O., 1921 (Department of Scientific and Industrial Research)
Kemm, W. C., *Events relative to the town and inhabitants of Amesbury, Wilts. collated from slips written by William Cove Kemm of Amesbury (B.1813–D.1893)*, collated by Philip Dyke, 1970 (typescript in W.A. & N.H.S. Library, Devizes)
Kite, E., 'Notes on Amesbury monastery, with an account of some discoveries on the site in 1860,' in *Wiltshire Notes & Queries* iii (1899–1901), pp. 114–119, 145–154, 221–227, 258–267, 289–305, 354–366, 433–447
Kite, E., 'Amesbury monastery,' in *Wiltshire Notes & Queries* iv (1902–1904), pp. 74–80, 124–138
Knowles, D., *The Monastic order in England*, Cambridge: Cambridge Univ. Press, 2nd edition, 1963
Lewis, R. A., 'County government since 1835,' in *Victoria History of Wiltshire* v (1957), pp. 231–292
Longmate, N., *The Workhouse*, London: Maurice Temple Smith, 1974

Marsh, H., *Dark age Britain*, Newton Abbot: David & Charles, 1970
Mawer, A., & Stenton, F. M., *The Place-names of Worcestershire*, Cambridge: Cambridge Univ. Press, 1927 (English Place-Name Society, vol. 4)
Moon A., 'Old railway lines,' in Guthrie (1977), pp. 28—31
Moore, N., 'Amesbury Abbey: an introduction to its buildings past and present,' in *Hatcher Review* i (1976), pp. 26—35
Morris, J., *The Age of Arthur: history of the British Isles 350—650*, London: Weidenfeld & Nicolson, 1973
Oswald, A., *Clay pipes for the archaeologist*, Oxford: British Archaeological Reports, 1975 (B.A.R.14)
Parker, N., 'Military influence on Salisbury Plain,' in Guthrie (1977), pp. 24—27
Pevsner, N., *Wiltshire*, Harmondsworth: Penguin, 2nd edition, revised by Bridget Cherry, 1975 (The Buildings of England)
Pugh, R. B., (ed.) *Calendar of Antrobus deeds before 1625*, Devizes: W.A. & N.H.S. Records Branch, 1947 (W.A. & N.H.S. R.B.iii)
Pugh, R. B., 'The Early history of the manors in Amesbury,' in *Wiltshire Archaeological Magazine* lii (1947—1948), pp. 70—110
Pugh, R. B., 'The Abbey, later priory, of Amesbury,' in *Victoria History of Wiltshire* iii (1956), pp. 242—259
Pugh, R. B., (ed.) *Wiltshire goal delivery and trailbaston trials 1275—1306*, Devizes: Wiltshire Record Society, 1978 (W.R.S. xxxiii)
Ruddle, C. S., 'Early tobacco pipes,' in *Wiltshire Notes and Queries* i (1893—1895), pp. 281—282
Scott, R., 'Medieval agriculture,' in *Victoria History of Wiltshire* iv (1959), pp. 7—42
Short guide to the abbey church of St. Mary and St. Melor, (Amesbury), N.D. (1978)
Soul, J., *Amesbury old and new: reminiscences and reflections*, Salisbury: (Salisbury Times), N.D. (1923)
Soul, J., *Amesbury historic and prehistoric*, Salisbury: Salisbury Times, 1926
Stenton, F. M., *Anglo-Saxon England*, Oxford: Clarendon Press, 3rd. edition, 1971
Stevens, E. T., *Jottings on some objects of interest in the Stonehenge excursion*, Salisbury: Brown & Co., 1882
Stone, J. F. S., *Wessex before the Celts*, London: Thames & Hudson, 1958 (Ancient Peoples and Places)
Talbot, C. H., 'Amesbury monastery,' in *Wiltshire Notes & Queries* iii (1899—1901), pp. 549—556, iv (1902—1904), pp. 11—20
Thody, D. W. J., 'Railway reveries,' in *Wiltshire Industrial Archaeology* v (1974), pp. 35—42
Turner, G. L. *Original records of early nonconformity under persecution and indulgence*, London: Unwin, 1911
Webb, S., & B., *English poor law history*, London: Longman, 4 vols., 1929
Webster, G., & Dudley, D. R., *The Roman conquest of Britain AD 43—57*, London: Pan Books, revised edition, 1973 (British Battles Series)
Wesley, J., *Journals*, vol. 4 London: Dent, 1909
Willoughby, R. H. W., 'Revd. Thomas Holland, a mechanical genius,' in *W.A. & N.H.S. Bi-annual Bulletin* 10 (March 1971), pp. 10—11
Windley, E. J., *Amesbury: its abbey, its church and its saint*, Leighton Buzzard: Faith Press, 3rd impression, 1917
Youings, J., *The Dissolution of the monasteries*, London: Allen & Unwin, 1972 (Historical Problems Series)

INDEX

Abbey (979—1177): 1, 6, 7—8, 10—1, 13, 39
Abbey (1177—1539): *see* Priory
Abbey Church: 1, 8, 10, 13—4, 16, 23, 38, 54, 74—87, 92, 110
Abbey Lane: 100
Abbey Mansion: 1, 13—4, 22, 23, 25, 28, 90, 92—4
Abbey Square: 95
Addison, Joseph: 38
Aelfthryth, *Queen* [Elfrida]: 7—8
Aethelred, *King*: 7
Aethelstan, *King*: 7, 8
Alfred, *King*: 8
Allington: 10, 58, 123
Almanaze Path: 94
Ambri [Ambre]: 5
Ambrius: 15—6
Ambrosius Aurelianus: 5, 6, 15, 86
Amesbury Earls (manor): 16—7, 22, 44, 61, 97
Amesbury Electric Light Company: 55, 100
Amesbury Fire Brigade: 36, 114, 119, 121—2
Amesbury Friendly Society: 97
Amesbury Heaver: 29
Amesbury Highway Board: 32
Amesbury House: 113, 118, 126
Amesbury Parish Council: 57, 90
Amesbury Priors (manor): 16—7, 20, 22, 31, 61, 97
Amesbury Psalter: 82.
Amesbury Rural District Council: 122
Andover: 7, 34, 35, 55
Andrews, Edwin: 25
Antrobus Arms Hotel: 23, 24, 94—5
Antrobus family: 23, 24, 39, 82, 84, 113
Antrobus House: 23, 57
Antrobus Road: 23
Antrobus, *Sir* Edmund (2nd bart.): 23—5, 92, 100
Antrobus, *Sir* Edmund (3rd bart.): 39, 57
Antrobus, *Sir* Philip: 92
Arcade, The: 113.
Arthur, *King*: 15, 86

Asher family: 24
Aubrey, John: 30, 31
Avon Buildings: 122
Avon, River: 1, 2, 3, 6, 9, 28, 40, 44, 50, 54, 71, 89, 119
Avon Temperance Hotel: 94
Avon Valley: 3, 5, 6, 9, 29, 43, 49, 64
Avonstoke Close: 50
Back Lane: 20, 33, 39, 109, 113
Bakehouse Lane [Bakers Lane]: 33, 36, 58, 100, 113, 123
Balet, John and Christine: 17
Barnard [Bartnett] Field: 17, 27, 58
Batho, George Best: 24, 106
Battle of the Nile Clumps: 46, 70—1
Bayley, Gabriel: 30
Beacon Hill: 31, 40, 47, 63, 90
Bear Inn: 94
Beatrice, *Abbess:* 11.
Becket, *Saint* Thomas: 10, 14.
Bedford, Duke of: 30, 31
Bedwyn: 9
Beggar's Opera: 23
Bell Hotel: 20, 126
Birdcage Row: 126
Birdlimes Farm, Porton: 37
Bishop, William: 119
Black Cross Field: 17, 27, 58
Blake, John: 25
Blatch, Mr.: 99
Bloxham, Dr. Robert: 95
Blue Lion Inn: 40
Bocker Mead: 61
Boneser, Joe: 122
Boney Mead: 91, 99
Bonnewe, Florence: 21
Boscombe: 10
Boscombe Down: 6, 17, 40, 44, 66
Boscombe Road: 28
Bowles Hatches: 29
Bremhill: 21
Brigmerston: 2
Bristol Aeroplane Company: 119
Brittany: 7—8, 15
Broad Bridge: 72
Browne, Caroline: 39

132

Bruce family: 22
Bugden's Motor Cycle Depot: 109, 112
Bulford: 3, 5, 10, 31, 32, 40, 58, 63, 64, 66, 69, 119
Bus Station: 114, 117, 126
Butterfield, William: 74—9, 81, 83—4
"Butts, Les": 88, 98
Cantilupe (manor): 17
Carleton, *Lord*: 22
Carpenter Street: 20
Cemetery Corner: 71—3
Centre, The: 109—13
Childs, Asa: 99, 100, 103
Chimes House: 55, 100—2
Chippenham: 21
Chitterne: 31, 32
Cholderton: 59, 63
Chopping-Knife Inn: 35, 94—5
Choulston: 10
Christ the King School: 58
Church Lane: 54, 94
Church Street: 6, 55, 88, 91—7
Cinema: 55, 113—4, 116
Clarence family: 16
Clarendon Forest: 20
Clarke, William and Margaret: 20
Cobbett, William: 29, 35
Coldharbour: 17, 36, 68—9, 110, 115, 119
Cole, Quint: 122
Colonial Restaurant: 61
Comilla House: 31, 32, 61—2, 109, 111
Coneybury Hill: 17
Conyger, The (manor): 17
Cook, Thomas: 38
Cooper family: 24
Co-operative Stores: 113, 117, 119
Corsham: 21
Coster, Farmer: 99
Countess Farm and Field: 16, 17, 24, 25, 27, 28, 59—60, 98
Countess Road: 28, 31, 32, 58—63, 66, 68, 72, 111, 112
Cox, William: 38
Cread, Elizabeth: 25
Crooked Covert Copse: 110
Cuckold Hill: 98
Cursus, The: 2, 88
Dark Lane: 58, 98
Darrell, Joan: 21
Dawbeney, Robert: 12—4
Dawbeney's (manor): 17
Dawbeney's Mill: 44, 71
Despencer family: 16
Devizes: 30, 32, 53, 58
Diana House: 22, 61—2
Donhead: 21
Drove, The: 63, 68
Druids Lodge: 40
Druids Restaurant: 61
Dunkirk Veterans Club: 94
Dunstan, *Archbishop*: 7

Durnford Track: 44, 49, 50, 123.
Durrington: 21, 64
Durrington Walls: 2, 5
Earls Court Farm and Fields: 16, 17, 25, 28, 36, 58, 98, 99
Earls Court Road: 36, 58, 113
Earls Farm Down: 3, 5
East Field, West Amesbury: 17
East Kennett: 32
Edgar, *King*: 7
Edmiston Road: 123
Edward I, *King*: 12, 16
Edward, Saint, *King* and Martyr: 7—8
Edward the Confessor, *King*; 9, 10
Edwards, Job: 14, 83, 113, 114
Edwards Road: 113
Eleanor of Provence, *Queen*: 12, 15
Elfrida, *Queen* [(Aelfthryth]: 7—8
Elm Hays Field: 94
Enford: 24
Eyers, William: 25
Eyres family: 24, 106
Fairholme: 39, 95
Fairlawn: 106
Fairs: 20, 33, 58, 64, 88, 94, 113, 123
Fields, Betty: 114
Figheldean: 2, 10
Fire Station: 119, 121—2
Fisherton Anger: 3
Fittleton: 31
Flitcroft Atlas: 17, 27
Florak, Pontius: 16
Flower, Edward: 38, 39
Flower Lane: 20, 36, 72, 97, 119—20, 122, 123
Folly Bottom: 47, 63, 68
Fovant House: 106
Fowle, Fulwar W.: 24, 37, 38
Fox, Edward: 30
Frog Lane: 20, 72, 97, 122
Gallows Hill: 71
Gane, Joseph: 25
Gauntlet family: 30—1, 103
Gay, John: 22—3
Geneville, Isabel de: 75
Geoffrey of Monmouth: 15—6
George Hotel: 20, 24, 31, 32, 102—3, 105
Gilbert, Fanny: 25
Godric. 15
Grately: 40
Great Durnford: 3, 9, 50, 64, 71, 72
Great South Ham Field: 17
Grey Bridge: 14, 60—1, 94
Greyhound Inn: 113, 115
Guinevere, *Queen*: 6, 15—6, 83
Half Borough Field: 17, 27
Ham Hatches: 29, 71, 72
Haradon Hill: 6, 63
Harrison, John: 100
Harrison, Richard: 39
Harrow Way: 2, 3
Hayes [Hays] family: 94, 97

133

Hayward, Mr.: 98
Henry II, *King*: 10—1, 12
Henry VIII, *King*: 21
Hertford, Earl of [Edward Seymour]: 22, 61
Heytesbury: 31
Hicks, Mr.: 109
High Street: 1, 6, 20, 36, 38, 55, 96, 100—9, 111, 119
Highfield Road: 58
Hillary Joseph: 25
Holders Road: 66—7, 68, 90
Holland, Thomas: 36, 37, 83, 122
Hopper, Thomas: 92
Hough, William: 106
Hutchins, Mr.: 99
Idmiston: 58
Ivydene: 36, 113—4, 116—7, 119, 122
Jockey Inn: 38, 106
Kemm, William: 14, 31, 33, 103
Kemm's Square: 126
Kent House: 22, 28, 61—3, 94, 100
Kenton, Anthony Cook: 106
Kent's Chamber: 84
Kilford family: 24
Kings Arms Inn: 95, 97, 100
Kings Island: 29, 44, 98
Kintbury Abbey: 10
Kitchener Road: 63, 67, 68, 109—10
Lake: 49
Lake Down: 40
Lancaster family: 12, 16
Lancelot: 15
Larkhill: 31, 40, 66, 119
Lime Kiln Hill: 50
Little Field: 98
Little South Ham Field: 17
Lloyds Bank: 95, 97
Lock-up: 33, 100, 103, 110
London Road: 5, 28, 32, 44, 54, 61, 63—4, 66, 68—9, 111
Long, Ann: 25
Long, Thomas: 37
Long, William: 28
Lords Walk: 22, 61, 69, 89, 112
Louvain, nuns from: 23, 38
Lower Folds: 61
Lynchets Road: 58
Lynchets, The: 50, 57
Lynchfield Road: 58
Maddington: 10
Maggs, Joseph: 25
Malmesbury: 10, 21
Malory, *Sir* Thomas: 15
Market House: 33, 97, 99, 123
Market Place: 24, 33, 100, 123, 125—6
Markets: 20, 33, 34, 58, 64, 113
Marlborough: 21, 31, 95
Marlborough Downs: 2
Marlborough Road, Old: 49, 58
Marlborough Street: 20, 101
Martins Field: 98
Mary, *Princess*: 12, 16
Matravers, Agnes: 109

Melksham: 21
Melor, Saint: 6, 7—8, 13, 15—6, 20, 33, 81—2, 88
Merchant, Thomas: 39, 119
Mere: 21, 31
Merlin: 15—6
Methodist Chapels: 36, 38, 39, 101, 104, 122
Meyrick, Arthur: 39, 95
Middle Field, West Amesbury: 17, 27
Midland Bank: 103
Millards Cafe: 61
Milston: 2, 38
Moffatt, W. B.: 52
Monica, Sister: 38
Monk, Alfred: 83
Montagu family: 16
Montague, Sybil: 12—3
Moor Hatches: 29
Morris, Dr. Claver: 102
Mullens Pond: 31
Mundy family: 24
National School: 39, 126
Netheravon: 9, 36
Nevill family: 16
New Inn (former): 30, 31, 61—2, 100, 107, 109, 111
New Inn (present): 101
New Theatre Ballroom: 106
Newton Tony: 40, 58, 123
Nile Clumps: 46, 70—1
Normanton: 27, 31, 44, 71
Northams Close: 28, 99
Ogbury Camp: 3.
Old Grammar School [Rose's School]: 38, 39, 91, 106
Old Sarum: 3, 5, 16, 32, 56
"Olde Shoppe, Ye": 119, 126
Olding, Edmund: 25, 28
Olding, Joseph: 25
Osgood, John: 59, 99
Osmund: 10
Packway, The: 63
Pancet [Penchet]: 20
Park Farm: 25, 28, 61, 63
Parsonage Barn: 58
Parsonage Close: 58
Parsonage Lane: 58, 98
Parsonage Road: 58
Pewsey: 40, 64
Pewsey Vale: 5
Philpot, Mr.: 126
Phoenix House: 94
Pike family: 24, 26
Pinckney, Robert: 24, 28, 95, 99
Pink House School: 73, 91
Pitts Garage: 114
Police: 25, 51, 56, 110
Poore, Mr.: 99
Porton: 37, 44, 57, 99
Post Office: 32, 34, 106, 107, 108—9, 119
Pouncette Street: 16, 20

134

Pound, The: 99, 119
Priory (1177–1539): 12–5, 21, 22, 37, 39, 52, 74–6, 94, 95, 123
Purdue, Charles: 25
Purnell, Joseph: 24
Pyle, Dr. Charles: 24, 106
Queens Fall Weir: 91
Queensberry Bridge: 23, 32, 72, 91–2
Queensberry, Catherine, Duchess of: 22–3
Queensberry, 3rd Duke of [Charles Douglas]: 22–3, 24, 27, 32
Queensberry, 4th Duke of [William Douglas]: 23, 32, 35, 99–100
Queensberry Hotel: 126
Railways: 32, 40, 64–6
Randall, Edward: 122
Ratfield Down: 44
Ratfyn: 2, 38, 44, 58, 66
Ratfyn Farm: 17, 24, 25, 28, 64, 99
Ratfyn Road: 69
Rattue family: 24
Rawlings, Mary: 24
Recreation Ground: 71, 90
Red House Farm: 25, 28, 56, 99
Rede, John: 37
Redworth House: 122
Robinson, chemist: 106
Rolfe family: 24
Rollestone: 40, 66
Roman Catholic Church: 69
Rooke, Michael: 25
Rose, John: 38
Rose's School [Old Grammar School]: 38, 39, 91, 106
Ruddle, Charles: 84
Rushall: 32
Rushworth, Patience: 24
Saint Melor: 6, 7–8, 13, 15–6, 20, 33, 81–2, 88
Salisbury: 1, 5, 21, 30, 32, 34, 36, 49, 58, 64, 66, 114, 119
Salisbury, Earls of: 16
Salisbury Plain: 1, 2, 40, 45, 64
Salisbury Road: 17, 50, 53, 55–7, 58, 68, 99, 119
Salisbury Street: 6, 20, 33, 36, 55, 96, 97, 100, 103, 109, 110, 119, 122, 123–6
Sandell family: 25, 38, 91, 101
Saracens Head Inn: 97
Saucer, Robert: 20
Saxon Cross: 84–6
Scanes, Farmer: 98
School (now Junior School): 39, 110
School Lane: 20, 39, 56, 109–10, 113
Selfe, Henry: 25, 28
Seymour family: 22, 92
Shaftesbury: 8, 21, 37
Shallow Water Meadow: 99
Shrewton: 31, 40, 63, 64
Sloan's Garage: 31, 103, 106
Smith, Robert: 30

Smithfield Street: 20, 36, 113–9
Smokey Joe's: 61
Somerset, 4th Duke of: 22
Somerset, Protector [Edward Seymour]: 22
Soper, Walton: 103
Soul, John: 97
South Ham Farm and Field: 17, 20, 27, 28
South Mill: 24, 25, 45, 49, 50, 53–5, 58, 72
South Mill Hill: 3, 24, 35, 45, 46, 50, 51, 100
South Mill Hill Field: 17, 99
South Mill Road: 50, 53, 56, 123
Southams Close: 28
South's (manor): 17
Spratt, Henry: 38, 39
Spredbury family: 24, 94
Stallard, William: 109
Stonehenge: 2, 15, 16, 28, 31, 33, 40, 46, 56, 66, 88, 90, 95, 102
Stonehenge Avenue: 46
Stonehenge Road: 3, 54, 71–3, 91, 122
Stonehenge Temperance Hotel: 104
Summer Field: 98
Swan Inn: 20, 30, 31, 126
Tanner, Thomas: 25, 28
Tanners Lane: 36, 72, 100, 119, 122
Three Cups Inn: 20
Three Tuns Inn: 101
Thruxton: 31
Tilshead: 9
Tollhouses: 32, 50, 56, 58, 60, 72–3, 91, 122
Totterdown: 1
Town End Little Field: 17, 98, 110
Townsend Mill: 50, 54
Trowbridge, John: 29
Truckle family: 24, 26
Tucker, Frank: 109, 111–2
Turner, Mary: 25
Turnpike Trusts: 23, 31–2, 56, 76, 102
Ugford: 16
Upavon: 2
Upper Folds: 61
Vespasian's Camp: 2–5, 17, 70, 2
Vicarage (former): 14, 24, 94, 95
Vicarage (present): 94, 95
Vincent, Widow: 101
Viney, Ann: 26
Viney's Farm: 25, 57
Wanborough: 21
Warne, William: 98
Washington, *Sir* Lawrence: 44
Webb, John: 23, 92
Wesley, John: 38
West Amesbury: 17, 20, 27–8, 31, 37, 38, 44, 46, 49, 50, 64, 71–2
West Field, West Amesbury: 17, 27
Westbury: 40, 64
Wherewell Abbey: 7
White Hart Inn: 106

Whitnam Bank: 99
William of Malmesbury: 15
Willoughby Hedge: 31
Wilsford: 5, 49
Wilton: 8, 10, 16, 21, 37, 55
Wilts. & Dorset Bank: 109
Wiltshire, William: 109
Winterbourne Bassett: 10
Winterbourne Gunner: 49
Winterslow: 10
Wittenham Path: 54, 72–3, 91

Wood Way: 72, 123
Woodford: 2, 49, 50, 64
Woodhenge: 1, 44, 47
Woods, "Bungy": 54, 55, 69, 91
Workhouse: 24, 25, 26, 29, 35–6, 50–3, 55
Wrestler's Gate: 31
Wylye: 31
Wyndersham House: 39
Yarham, Misses: 101, 104
Zillwood family: 14, 38, 39, 126

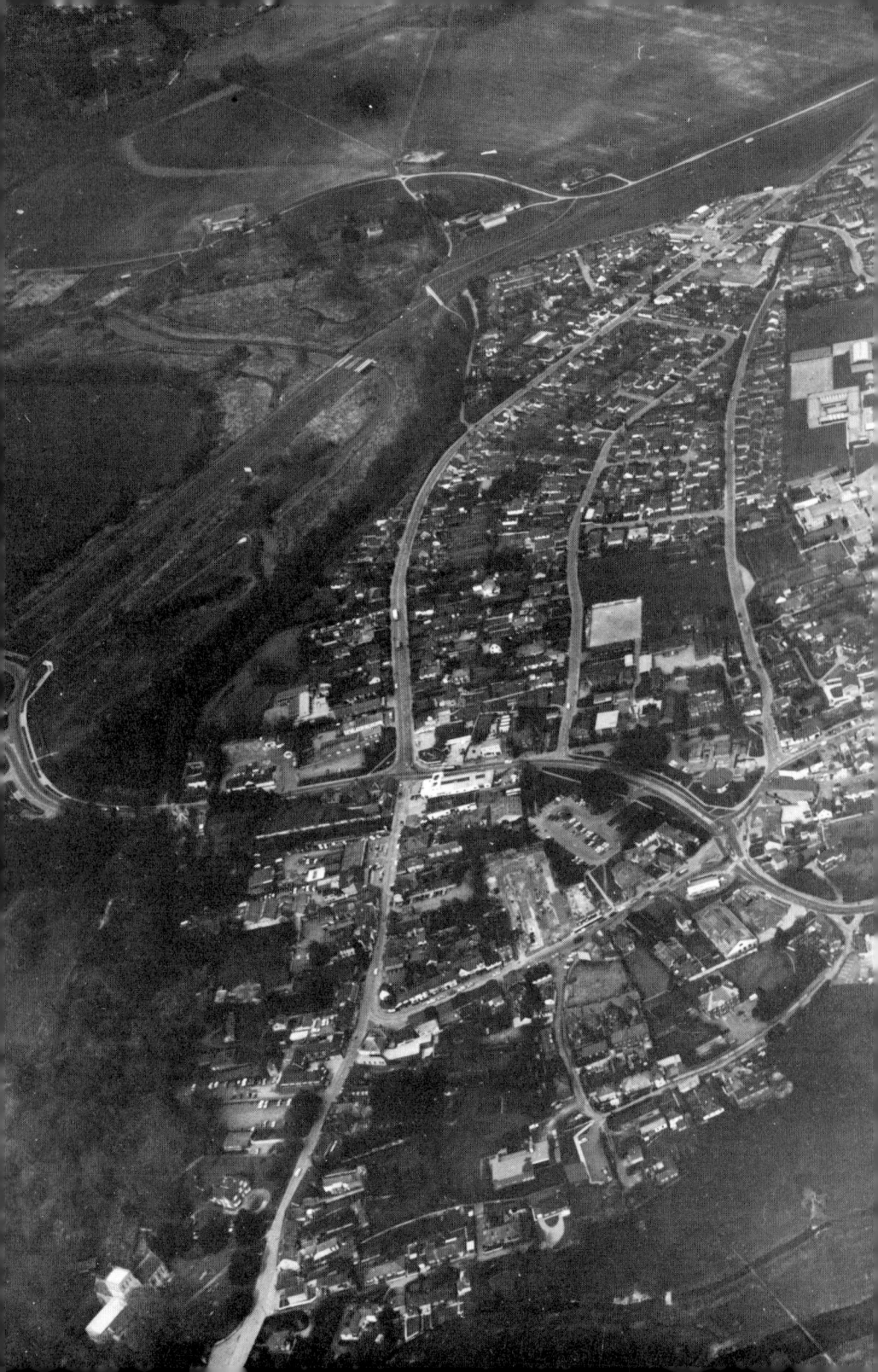